ADVERTISING PROFITS FROM HOME

VISIONARY STRATEGIES

Advertising Profits From Home

Published by: Visionary Strategies
Copyright © 2009

Printed in the United States of America
First Printing July of 2009

Neither the author nor Visionary Strategies, Inc., in any way make any warranty, guaranty or representation, expressed or implied, as to the potential volume, profits, or success of any activity or undertaking described herein.

All information related to the potential to earn money or realize a profit from any activity described herein was received from third parties and was not created or verified by the author or Visionary Strategies, Inc., or any agent of either of them.

Neither the author nor Visionary Strategies, Inc., in any way warrant or confirm the accuracy of any information provided herein.

The reader should conduct an independent investigation into the information contained herein before taking any action.

The success or failure of any undertaking described herein or based on information provided herein may involve financial risks solely dependent upon the reader's own ability and efforts, changes in technology or shifts in market realities.

Finally, nothing contained herein should be construed as legal advice.

Regulations vary from state to state, and change from time to time.

Consult your own independent legal counsel as to the legality of any undertaking before taking action based on information contained herein.

Cover Design: Freddy Solis
Interior Design: Tressa Foster
Production Management: Dean Enterprises LLC

Dedication

This book is dedicated to family.

Any success I enjoy in life is a direct result of one man; my incredible father who has influenced me my entire life. He has always believed in me, and taught me what I need to know to be successful, both as a person and in business. There is no doubt that I would not be able to write this book, nor would I have succeeded in Affiliate Marketing, without his guidance, knowledge and trust. By showing me that anything is possible if I set my mind on it, and teaching me how to persevere and constantly strive for success, my father made this book possible.

At the age of 15, my father took responsibility for the financial security of his family. His amazing work ethic was instrumental in his successful business ventures throughout life. But he always gave back and helped many people along the way. He continues to be an inspiration and guiding force in our family. My goal is to someday look back on my life and know that I lived it in exactly the way he wanted; that I had earned his respect. Thankfully, I've always had his love.

Though I was lucky to delve into the Web right when it became a force in our lives, I could never have progressed as I did without my father's support. He created an opportunity for me; providing computer and Web access, as well as encouragement, in leaning how to use the Web for business. Even when some of my ideas were a bit "out there," he offered support, whether he agreed with my idea or not.

He currently works with me, reminding me of business ideas and concepts that never change. Whether in traditional media or on the Web, certain business tools and basic concepts will never change, and my father is a constant reminder of my desire to be the best at what I do. I could not continue to be successful without reminders and advice that create the core of a successful business person…and this comes from my dad.

It's important that my father and I acknowledge the influence of my mother in both our lives. My dad will readily tell you how lucky he is to have her. My mom has always supported me, stood up for me, and taught me how to live as a better person, helping others and giving back. I, too, am so lucky to have her, and I wouldn't be who I am today without her constant reassurance and support.

To my sister, Brittain, I appreciate everything you do for me, and I love you very much. To my brother, Adrian, you are a great brother, student, and now a very successful businessman. Continue doing what you are doing, and always strive to be better, I love you very much.

To my grandmother, "Nanny," you are amazing! You have shown me that, no matter what happens in life, one must always smile and continue living your life, being thankful for everything you have.

To my Uncle Lynn and Aunt Julie, thank you for all of your support and love. You have both been an integral part of my success by always being there for me and believing in me and the things I have wanted to do.

To Josh, my best friend. Thank you for all your support and guidance. It's rare in life to find someone you can completely trust with everything you have. I am very lucky that you have been not only a great friend, but also a great business partner. You have been instrumental in making everything I do a success. I owe much of my success to you, and not a day goes by that I don't appreciate everything you do for me.

Success is possible by surrounding yourself with people who are positive, motivating, and inspiring. My entire family has been exactly that for me, and I owe my success to them all.

Thank you all for your continued support. I love you all.

Contents

Introduction

When I started writing *Advertising Profits from Home,* the economy was basically a complete disaster. Banks were closing or being bought out by larger, more stable financial institutions, people were losing their jobs or taking pay cuts almost every day and new government bailouts were taking place weekly. We actually saw the failure of *Chrysler* and *General Motors*, two of America's largest and oldest companies. The economic crisis we are facing is changing our country as we know it. Not only are we facing volatility in the stock market and housing market, we are also seeing companies that were household names file for bankruptcy, close down or vanish. We have seen a record number of foreclosures, a horrible credit crises, and banks that will not lend money.

By the time this book finds its way into your hands, there is a good chance that this crisis will have become even worse. I recognize that the state of the economy has everyone, including you, feeling depressed and worried. People all over the country are struggling, wondering how they will pay their bills.

Here's some good news: You are reading my book at the perfect time. I am going to share the knowledge and techniques I use to generate a steady income using the Internet. Right now there are more people online than ever before, and your time to cash in on it is **RIGHT NOW**.

Think about this for just one second. When was the last time you saw the headline *"Internet Companies Failing by the Dozens as Economic Crisis Worsens* ?" What was the last Internet company to collapse as a result of the current economic situation? Have you heard anything about Internet-based business' failing on the national news channels? The answer to these questions is no, none, it's not happening.

Even though economic conditions are worsening, the Internet continues to grow at a record pace. If you were just laid off from work, are you going to take a vacation? More than likely, you will be vacationing in your own backyard! Are you going to go out every weekend and shop and have fancy dinners? Only if you consider pizza to be a fancy dinner! Let's say you didn't lose your job, but you're worried about the possibility of losing it or having to take a pay cut. Are you going to do these things? Probably not. The fact of the matter is, almost everyone is either losing their job, or doesn't feel their job is secure. This means major cutbacks in *"non-essentials,"* such as entertainment, travel, shopping, fine dining, driving, and almost anything else that isn't related to paying bills. A tightening of our belts is essential to everyone's financial survival.

With all of that in place, people simply just stay home more now than they used to. Quick question; what do most people spend their time doing when they are at home? If you guessed watching TV, you're wrong. If you guessed getting on the Internet, YOU'RE RIGHT! There are millions and millions of people spending more and more time online, rather than doing the things they used to do. There simply is no shortage of Internet customers.

In this book, I am going to show you how to cash in on the Internet by using proven strategies and techniques that make money every single day. There are plenty of customers online, and as long as you have the determination to succeed and the knowledge to make it work, you can create your dream business.

You are going to hear real life stories from people just like you, who decided they wanted more out of life, used my techniques and are now generating money on the Internet. It's time for you to decide that your 9-to-5 job isn't giving you all you want out of life. It's time to take action, get out there, and create your own business online, and with the help of my techniques and strategies. You can do just that with the help of this book.

I am not a self-labeled *"guru."* In fact, I hate the term. I am no different than you, excepts that I have learned how to make money online. I am not someone who *"used to make money ten years ago"* and now just teaches those things that used to work. Ten years ago, I was sixteen and just starting to drive! I am, however, someone who is doing this right now, learning more each and every day, and aspiring to become an even more successful Internet entrepreneur. You're learning from someone that's making money **RIGHT NOW**. I will show you how to take the fast track to success, avoid making mistakes, and come out with a great income stream from the Internet. This could be the most important book you will ever read in your entire life.

Decide Who You Are Right Now

Are you the person who's going to read a few pages of this book put it down, and forget about it? Go back to your everyday routine and just let this opportunity pass you by? Are you the person who's going to read all the negative baloney about how Internet businesses don't work and then just give up? It's important right now for you to decide that this is not who you are going to become. Don't let the negative people in your life cause you to miss out on your opportunity for success. In my opinion, that would be an absolute travesty.

Or are you the one who's going to read this book and study it as if it were one of your college course books? Are you the person who's going to put the techniques to use? Are you the person who's going to stay focused on success and follow steps to achieve just that? If so, then by the time you finish this book, you will have the knowledge, wisdom, and capabilities to be successful and profitable with an Internet business.

Let me be your teacher for the next few hundred pages, and I promise you will gain the knowledge and confidence you need to be successful online, and change your life forever in the process. Who you are is your choice, but think about this: if you choose to not read this book, what are you going to use to get ahead and when are you going to do it?

If you happen to be near a computer, take a few minutes right now and go to:

www.anthonymorrison.com/intro

Watch the short video I put together just for you. I think it will help you prepare for the success you want. (If you can't view the video right now, that's fine, just make sure you do it before finishing this book.)

Right now is **YOUR MOMENT** to succeed. Let's get started…

SECTION I
THE WHO AND WHY OF THIS BOOK

CHAPTER 1

The Goal, the Plan & the Tools

Why are you here, right now, reading this first sentence in this book? You're here because you have a goal. You're looking for a plan to reach that goal, and the tools to implement that plan to insure its success. My goal is solely to give you all of the information that you need in the pages of this book, and to do it in such a way that it will eliminate all possibilities of failure when it comes to achieving your goal.

Your Goal is My Mission

It's OK to say it; you want to make money, and you want to make money now, not at some point in the nebulous future. Unless you're planning on spending the rest of your life in a monastery, money is necessary. It's a lofty calling, living a life of service, but for the rest of us, we need to pay the rent or the mortgage, eat a relatively healthy diet, care for our family, and even have a little fun along the way.

You may be close to achieving your goals, you may be falling behind, or even hitting rock bottom financially. Wherever you are at in your personal journey, you can't "read my lips," but you can read the following: In these pages, I will give you a plan and the tools to make it happen. This plan and these tools will help you reach your financial security goals, have some fun, and do it in a way that is enjoyable, ethical and beneficial to others. This is my promise to you.

The Method

The methods we will use to achieve financial well-being are encompassed in the term *"Internet Affiliate Marketing."* I have personally made millions of dollars using it, and I know that you can, too. This book can make it happen, even if:

- you're falling behind on bills
- you only have an elementary education
- you have never run a business before
- ideas about making money don't wake you up at night
- you have little or no seed money for a new venture

None of these factors matter, as affiliate marketing on the Internet is just like the Wild West frontier in the 1800's. There is *"gold in them thar' hills!"* But there is one big difference. While the gold rush involved wagons and horse racing in the fierce competition for riches,

- you'll have a team dedicated to your success in affiliate marketing
- this team won't charge you any money for most of their help
- unlike hoping that there is any gold under the ground on your claim, you are assured that there is profit in affiliate marketing if you just follow my plan.
- you can sit comfortably in your home and mine your riches, with no travel or inventory required.

The Plan

I will share with you exactly how affiliate marketing works: the structure, the players, and how you can make as much money as you want from the comfort of your home with the time you have available to you. I'll disclose the motivation behind each of the players on your team, and how to use *their* motivations to reach *your* goals.

Your plan, much like a treasure map, will lay out the path, help you to avoid the hazards, and guide you to the *"X"* that marks the spot where riches are available to anyone who has the motivation and desire to succeed and can follow my simple instructions. It isn't about education, nor is it about intelligence. You're not starting a factory, so a huge capital investment isn't necessary. You don't need previous business experience, or even management or business training.

The plan I am about to present to you here is precisely the plan I would use for myself if I were starting an affiliate marketing business today. You'll see it in its refined state, already *"road-tested"* from my experiences over the years. With this plan, you can start receiving checks and direct deposits in weeks, and you will not need inventory, support phone numbers or staff wages to turn a profit. You will wake up every morning eager to see both the activity in your affiliate accounts, and the dollars that accumulated while you were sleeping.

My plan gives you everything you need to know to create a 24/7 business that operates world-wide by allowing you to be a resource for customers for literally tens of thousands of products and services. You won't have to handle any of them, nor will you have to warranty or support them. You will only be responsible for directing a willing customer to a vendor for a purchase. Actually, some of your best income will come from customer referrals who may NEVER buy anything!

The Tools

I won't just give you a plan and leave you alone to manage it, you will be provided with all of the companies, contacts and resource tools that you will need to implement your plan. There will not be a single plan item that doesn't include everything you will need to be successful. You will be given the following valuable resources:

- Affiliate marketing networks
- Tools to compare payouts and make decisions
- Web site and blog tools to build your Internet presence
- Definitions & terminology you'll need to know
- Payout negotiation strategies
- Demographic tools to identify excellent markets with little competition
- Advertising methods, media and strategies

There's a lot more, but I want you to see that my mission is to turn you into a successful Internet affiliate marketer using the method, plan and tools in this book. All you need is the motivation and desire to use what I provide, and follow through with this method for a successful and financially rewarding business.

What Qualifies Me to Be Your Mentor?

Wondering who I am is a valid question. You're on the first chapter of a book that promises to motivate and teach you how to change your life using the Internet and affiliate marketing. It's only fair, and quite important, that you are comfortable with my credentials and expertise. What better way is there to acquaint you with my background than to tell you a bit about myself and how I've made millions of dollars in the affiliate marketing business?

The theme of this book will beevident to you pretty quickly. It will be reinforced with examples of my childhood businesses and later success on the Internet. The fact that you can read this book shows that you are capable of success. If you read it through and put the information to use, there is no limit to what you can accomplish. It isn't only education, or life experience, or even intelligence that will make you successful.

As I said before, you don't need to be a person of means; your current financial situation, no matter what it is, is not a deterrent to success. I'll share with you a story about my first experience at seven years of age. It shows that education and experience aren't critical to success. After all, how much education and experience could a seven year old possibly have? Read on and you will find out. Then, I'll share my family's *"riches to rags"* experience to illustrate that financial hardship can be a motivator, not a deterrent. So watch for the frequent illustrations of the *"you can do this"* theme throughout the book, and you'll have a full understanding of the one critical requirement for success … motivation.

Money has never been the ultimate goal for me; neither has it been the inspiration to create a new business. Money is necessary, and there are many wonderful things in life that are only possible with money. But, without passion, money is not enough to give me the drive and determination to make a business successful.

So, begin your journey to financial rewards with *"Internet Affiliate Marketing"* knowing that you can be successful in many ways. Your greatest success will come from enjoying what you do, and having a passion for the service you're providing.

Learning What's Important

My parents were financially well-off; my father made millions of dollars over the years in real estate investment. I attended a private school through 12th grade, and my brother and I had enjoyable child-hoods. But, though our parents treated us well, they never wanted us to develop a sense of entitlement.

One Christmas after remote-control electric cars became popular, our parents bought us the entire line. However, they made it clear that we should give back as well. During the holidays, the local shopping mall set up a Christmas tree with hundreds of angels on it, each representing one underprivileged child. With our mom, we picked angels off the tree and shopped for gifts for each of the children. The point was made; there is a duty to show compassion for others less fortunate.

These lessons in giving back were supplemented by constant reinforce-ment of values, work ethic, and earning our way in life. My father's dad passed away when he was a child. As the eldest son, my father worked during his teen years to support his mother and siblings. He continued to support his mother until she passed away, and was determined to provide the best life he could for his family.

From an early age, our parents taught us to be respectful, compassion-ate and industrious. We had a comfortable life, but certain luxuries were available to us only if we found a way to earn the money to buy them. This set the tone very early in my life that I should learn to work for what I wanted, and that anything was possible if I wanted it badly enough.

My Early Experiences of Success

When I was just seven years old, I noticed that many of my friends' fami-lies had hot tubs, but we did not. When I approached my mother with this obvious and pressing need, she responded saying, *"If you want one so badly, why don't you work for the money and buy one?"* Of course, the first order of business was for her to explain the concept of *"work"* to me and how it could result in the purchase of a Jacuzzi.

She helped me grasp the idea that wanting something badly wasn't a means to an end; but, in wanting it badly enough, an enterprising seven-year-old could go out and find a way to earn the money to buy it. She didn't tell me how, but did make me believe that I could do it. My mother was a huge influence on my later success, because this  little lesson gave me the confidence that anything is possible, even for a seven-year-old boy. You just need to want it, and then apply your current knowledge and experience to a plan to get it.

So, what does a seven-year-old know about anything? What life experience is there to fuel an idea and a way to earn the money to buy a hot tub? Well, I knew what I liked, and one of the things I liked most was candy. And, I knew that all of my friends liked candy as well. It wasn't a great leap to decide that I should find a way to make the money I needed by selling candy.

I went to *Sam's Club*, bought some boxes of chocolate bars, and started selling them door to door. I didn't mind the work at all, but realized that it would be a much longer process if I didn't get some help. I convinced my brother and sister to get involved, paying them to go door to door as well. We worked our neighborhood, and then branched out to surrounding areas. Much to my mother's surprise, in three weeks we had earned the money to buy that Jacuzzi.

Of course, there was no stopping me after that experience. If I wanted something, I immediately put a plan into place, building a business to make it happen.

It was a year or so later that I decided I needed to buy a motorcycle for my father. He was a selfless person, always providing for the family, but rarely bought anything for himself if it wasn't an absolute necessity. At the time, his brother and several of his friends all had motorcycles and I overheard him telling my mother that he loved the idea of riding with my uncle on the weekends. That's all I had to hear, I launched my next business just to buy my father that motorcycle.

There's no better plan than utilizing proven methods and tactics, so I went back to *Sam's Club* and bought boxes and boxes of candy. At eight years old, I hit the streets again, selling the candy door to door. It only took a few weeks to earn more than $2,000, and I proudly presented my father with a *Honda*  *Shadow* motorcycle that he still has to this day.

Financing an Activity I Enjoyed

Those are examples of starting a business to realize a specific objective. My next business was simply a way to take a hobby to the next level. By financing that hobby, I was able to become more involved with something that I enjoyed. When you have a pastime that you love, it makes any related business that much more fun, and that generally that much more successful.

I was no different than a lot of boys my age, loving baseball and collecting baseball cards in my early teens. But there's a line between enthusiasm and obsession that I crossed pretty quickly. One indicator: I no longer was satisfied with just collecting cards that happened to come my way. I graduated to seeking out and purchasing hard-to-find baseball cards. This was definitely not an activity that my sensible parents would fund, so it was left to me to invent a new business to finance my obsession.

The timing was perfect and facilitated my plans. As a 13-year-old, I had a computer and Internet access just as the Web was being adopted by the masses. I participated in IM chat groups, widening my acquaintances to the nation, and even the world. It didn't take too long to realize that the Internet presented opportunities for the entrepreneur in me. On the Web, I was talking to card collectors around the world. I soon found that I could locate hard-to-find cards easily through the power of the *World Wide Web*.

I could also buy boxes of cards for less money on the Web than the local card shops paid their suppliers. While my friends were playing games on their computers, I was buying cards below wholesale, and reselling to the local shops. At that time, I was making $200 to $500 per month selling cards at thirteen. Of course, the card shop owners eventually caught on to the Internet, taking my middleman profit out of the picture, but it was a great run while it lasted.

There it is again! The theme of this book beautifully illustrated in one of my early experiences, and another opportunity for me to comment on entrepreneurs. I saw a chance to add value for the card shop owners by supplying them with inventory at a lower price. That's what entrepreneurial activity is all about. When that window of opportunity went away, so did the business. However, there wasn't a big overhead structure to dissolve. I turned my cards very quickly by not ordering product unless I knew I had a buyer. These types of situations present themselves every day to millions of people, but most don't recognize an opportunity when it's right in front of them, or don't have the confidence to pursue it.

When one door closes, another opens. When my card shop resale business evaporated, it wasn't a problem. I realized that there was an even greater opportunity to sell cards at the trade shows I had attended when buying cards for my collection. Again, I was in an environment I loved, dealing with baseball cards every day, and making money in the process.

I realized that the normal card vendors at these shows were older men, while the customer demographic was comprised of young boys. I *was* the consumer demographic, and the youngsters buying the cards felt more comfortable dealing with someone in their age group. With my father's support and transportation, we participated in five or more area trade shows each year. There were costs for the booth and space, but I was always aware of the minimum amount of sales that I needed to generate in order to break-even. A dice game I devised to draw traffic to my booth by giving cards as prizes was an effective tool to increase sales. Many trade show vendors still use this method today.

I didn't start this trade show baseball card sales business to get rich. Yes, I did need to turn a profit, but it was the next logical extension of my passion for baseball cards. That's one reason it was successful; I had the passion for the hobby and the business I generated was supporting it.

Getting rich with my hobby is not what I had in mind when I started this business, though it did provide a really nice income for a thirteen year old boy.

As others considered me an authority on baseball cards, my confidence grew and my age didn't matter. But there was something else I realized, and it became my first **Principle of Entrepreneurship: New Ideas Are All Around You**. Things you're passionate about are obviously one of the best sources of these ideas. But they can come from anywhere, or any activity in which you're engaged. Just keeping an open mind and paying attention can yield the next ultra-successful business idea.

The Five Personality Components of Entrepreneurial Thinking

Ideas that result in successful business ventures are everywhere, and I've come to realize that there are five personality components that spur entrepreneurial thinking and bring these ideas to the forefront for those who exhibit them.

Knowledge: Of course, it would be difficult to impossible to succeed at doing something about which you know nothing. Starting a new business without a thorough knowledge of your product or service is a bit like playing high stakes poker in Las Vegas without knowing the rules. The pros at the table will love you, but you'll leave with turned-out pockets. Knowledge of your subject, product, or service is necessary to any successful business venture and the more knowledge you have, the more successful your business will be.

Knowledge boosts your confidence, allowing you to analyze the benefits and the pitfalls of the business. One reason so many great businesses spring from hobbies or passions is that there is usually a substantial amount of personal knowledge that comes from being passionate about that topic or hobby. If you think you have a great business idea, but you're not in a comfortable position of knowledge, and then get the knowledge you need before you commit to the effort.

I'm going to provide a tremendous amount of information in this book. However, everyone is different, and each of us progresses at different speeds, with different help and support requirements. With this in mind, you have the option to have a personal coach to help you along your road to success. You don't need to go it alone, and you don't have to wonder if you've made the right decision at critical points in your plan. Just call 866-621-1532 (ext. 900), and someone will be there to provide the help, support and guidance you are looking for at any time

Confidence: Confidence is contagious. If you want prospective customers to feel confident that your products or services will fulfill their needs, then your self-confidence will go a long way toward giving them that feeling. Knowledge is an important factor. If you know your business, product or service, inside and out, you will convey a confident air and tone when talking or writing about it. I'm not referring to arrogance or false confidence. You really need to know your business, and you must honestly convey to others the fact that you do. We've already agreed that knowledge builds confidence. With the knowledge I'm bringing to you in this book, you'll go out into the affiliate marketing world with the confidence to follow your plan, build your business, and realize success.

Motivation: Have you ever known a successful businessperson who seemed to be losing their edge and their business? Complacency may have played a part in their demise. Becoming complacent when things are going well is a danger every businessperson faces. It's much easier to be highly motivated when you first start a business, as it's fresh, new and full of promise, even though you don't know what the next bend in the business road will reveal.

It's later, when you've been around a while, and you are possibly a bit bored with the day-to-day operation of the business that you are in danger of "death by complacency." Keeping your focus and motivation is critical to a successful and highly profitable business. I will show you how to avoid this complacency, and I'll share stories of how others have avoided complacency and grown their businesses.

Strategies: Try to think like a treasure hunter with an "X" marking the spot where the treasure is hidden. The map has a series of directions and landmarks to guide the hunter to the treasure, and there are pitfalls and dangers marked along the way as well. Following the route through the obstacles, around the quicksand, and staying away from the sheer cliffs is critical. Your business success is right where the "X" says it is, but developing a plan is the drawing of the map.

You must try to anticipate all of the things you must do, as well as all of the threats to success and competitive issues. This becomes your map to success and profits, but don't drop the ball by forgetting where you put the map. Keep it handy and follow it. Real people are using the strategies in this book to be successful entrepreneurs in the business world. I'm going to introduce you to them and share their stories of how they took the strategies they learned here and created their dream businesses.

Resourcefulness: Let's go back to our treasure map example. If it's a really old map, maybe there's been a few environmental changes over time, like an earthquake that has now created a chasm in the middle of the path not shown on the original map. The resourceful treasure hunter will find a way around it, or better yet, construct a makeshift bridge across it without a great delay in their hunt. Maybe there is a new quicksand field that didn't show on the map. Again, finding a dead tree and making a log bridge in order to get across the quicksand is the resourceful treasure hunter's solution to continuing on their path to riches. That's the way you have to think to succeed in business. When suddenly presented with a challenge or obstacle keeping you from executing your plan, don't turn around and leave with your marbles. Find a way to overcome it or get around it. Refusal to accept the barrier between you and the treasure is the same as refusing to accept *"no"* for an answer from a prospect client or customer. Just be persistent until *"no"* becomes *"yes."*

These five personality traits are the components of another **Principle of Entrepreneurship: Develop an Entrepreneurial Mindset**. Having a thorough knowledge of your business, maintaining your focus and motivation, developing strategies and a plan, following it, and being resourceful to overcome obstacles are all part of this mindset. When you see highly successful business people, they have this mindset, and you can as well. Again, it isn't higher education, nor is it intelligence or seed money that will make you successful.

Principle of Entrepreneurship: Be Aggressive

The words *"aggressive"* and *"annoying"* both start with the same letter, but being aggressive shouldn't require being annoying, although there are many business people who manage to be both. In my teens I moved from baseball cards into baseball memorabilia. I wanted to sell bats, hats, shirts, baseballs and other sports memorabilia, and knew that the value was in the autograph of the player on the item.

Using a strategic approach, I realized right away that sitting on a railing trying to catch a player leaving the stadium was an approach used by the masses, but it wasn't going to work for a business that required getting autographs on a lot of items by a lot of players. We began to take road trips for the weekend to catch double or triple-header games in a city. I would buy multiple baseball cards for players, hats, balls and bats before the trip, spending hundreds of dollars.

With a trailer full of this stuff, we'd head for the location of the game, but we didn't choose our hotel by amenities or cost. Instead, we chose a hotel where the players were staying. Arriving before the players, we'd be in the lobby when they checked in, listening carefully to hear their room numbers. Catching players in the hallways, lobbies and other areas of the hotel, my brother and I would ask each to sign multiple items. Many obliged without appreciable annoyance. Sometimes it took a bit more effort, and even a little luck, though luck is half the battle. Acting on it is the other half. Braves third baseman, Chipper Jones, didn't have a copy of his rookie baseball card, and really wanted one. Guess who did have one? He was happy to sign dozens of balls, bats and cards we had with us in exchange for that one card.

One problem collectors of sports memorabilia battle all the time is the ability to authenticate an autograph. Certificates of authentication are one approach. But, if I'm going to fake an autograph on a baseball, it's no more problem to fake one on a certificate saying the autograph is real. I knew that my profits would hinge on my ability to assure my customers of the authenticity of my autographs, so I carried a camera with me at all times, in order to snap a photo of the actual signing of the items. Sure, it's a bit aggressive to ask for an autograph and a photo to prove it, but it worked. Being aggressive certainly pays when it comes to business.

That statement isn't a platitude. An assertive approach is critical to your success in the affiliate marketing industry. I'll give you examples of just why it's so important I'll also share how others have used an aggressive approach to dramatically increase their income and build their businesses. Even when I was in my teens, I learned that being aggressive in business wasn't about annoying or alienating people. It is about asserting your knowledge and presenting your value, as well as not taking *"NO"* for an answer (in the right way).

Mustangs, Superchargers & OPM
(Other People's Money)

Once I turned fifteen, my love of baseball cards and sports memorabilia took a back seat to my desire for a car. Not just any. I fell in love with a 1996 Mustang GT. My parents knew by now that the cost of something I really wanted would not be an obstacle, so they encouraged me to get it if it was the car for me. Of course, they dutifully gave me all of the instructions for responsible driving, and made sure I knew that I didn't have to prove my car was fast by racing if challenged.

If you think I was obsessed with baseball cards, you can only imagine how intense I was about this car. I wanted to *know* that it was the fastest Mustang in the state of Mississippi, so I was compelled to get a supercharger. For those not into vintage cars and speed enhancements, a supercharger is a compressor that forces air into the combustion chambers creating a huge jump in power. There was only one little *"hitch"* in my plan to get a supercharger installed ASAP. It was the fact that this single part would cost me between $2000 and $3000. My parents helped me with the cost of the car and the insurance, but there was no way I was going to even attempt to approach them with this request.

I spent many hours on the Web and in chat rooms, learning about Mustangs and superchargers from thousands of Mustang enthusiasts. I would never have met these people without my computer and the Internet. Of course, with my Mustang passion came an idea. I started an online business matching supercharger buyers to sellers on the Web. I had the knack and resources to locate the parts that others couldn't so, I simply offered to get one for a buyer for $300 over the price I'd have to pay for it, and it worked!

Once I had an eager buyer and a willing seller, I would collect from the buyer, and send the money, less my commission, on to the seller. The seller would ship the supercharger directly to the buyer. I rarely saw the item, had no inventory, and had my first experience with making money by using OPM ("**O**ther **P**eople's **M**oney"). Basically, I had zero cost, no shipping costs, and a $300 profit. That's a business model I'll take any day. At fifteen, with no job, I was turning over twenty to thirty of these superchargers a year. I had no money of my own invested, no inventory, and was able to turn my 200 hp Mustang GT into an 800 hp racecar.

Are You In Financial Trouble? It's Not an Obstacle

I'm going to show you how to build a successful affiliate marketing business on the Internet without spending a lot of money. Your current financial situation shouldn't slow down your progress or dampen your motivation. I can say this without hesitation or doubt, as my own family's story will back me up 100%. It's a classic *"riches to rags"* story of a terrible financial calamity that took everything we had.

Encouraged and motivated by a respected local doctor, I had decided to attend college for a medical degree. This doctor, my pediatrician, was like a second father to me, and he helped people until the day he died. I was deeply influenced by his love of people and spirit of service, so medicine became my new passion. I had to drop all my other activities, including the supercharger business that was now in its third successful year. I was happily concentrating on pre-med and putting all my efforts into my education. Then, the unthinkable happened.

WorldCom and Fortunes Lost

By the time he retired at 65, my father had been successful in multiple careers. He had owned hotels, car dealerships, banks, condominiums and apartments. The millions he made should have made a solid foundation for a comfortable retirement, as well as fund his children's education. There was only one problem. He had placed the bulk of his money into *WorldCom* stock.

Though he had never been a big stock market investor, my father was comfortable with the fact that the world's second largest long distance carrier had their headquarters just minutes from where we lived. He put it this way: *"I feel comfortable investing in WorldCom. I can put my hands on it, I can see it, and I can stand inside the building."* He could not even have imagined that the ultimate collapse of the company was soon to come. With fraudulent accounting and overstated earnings and value, it was a quick death, with no chance for common stock holders to sell any of their holdings or to recoup any of their money. We lost everything we had.

We were now broke, unable to make the bills, and on the road to bankruptcy. Obviously, with no money for tuition, my medical education was going to have to be put on hold. Now a broken man, my father was no longer able to get work. He was *"unemployable"* due to his age. It was a dismal time, and someone had to step up to the plate and do *something*. One night, while studying, an idea came to me. There was no reason that I couldn't continue to sell Mustang parts online while still in school! To my surprise, when I called my father and pitched the idea, he shot it down. His knowledge of traditional business gave him the impression that it was an impossible task due to the up-front investment that he believed would be required.

I let his admonitions stop me for awhile as our financial situation worsened, with the last of our meager savings about to evaporate. Someone had to do something. So, I went against his advice and started *CoolBluePerformance.com*. With no credit or startup money, I knew this retail performance parts store was going to require some special effort and aggressive action. Using one of my dad's credit cards for startup costs, I found a Web site designer and hired her to design an auto parts store on the Web. It only took her a few days, and I was a business.

Looking at the thousands of competitors out there, I knew that it was going to take an innovative approach to make me stand out. I realized that not one of my competitors were open for business when a great many of their customers really needed to place a parts order. The competition had normal Eastern Standard Time business hours, and there was nobody available to speak to customers on the west coast after closing time on the east coast. Worse yet, people in other countries who wanted to order parts didn't have access to someone on the phone in their time zones.

Of course, there was only one response to this idea. *"We are open 24 hours a day, 7 days a week, for you to call and place your order."* I didn't work on corporate time. Instead, with a toll free number forwarded to my cell phone, I answered the phone whenever it rang. One of my biggest customers was from Australia. He was my customer because I answered the phone at 3 AM.

I didn't reinvent the wheel. I just made the existing wheel better. My auto parts weren't different or better, but they were available to thousands of people who had no easy access to customer service during their time schedule. *Cool Blue Performance* made $4800 in its first month, enough to pay the family bills.

CHAPTER 2

Why People Fail or Never Truly Succeed

This chapter isn't meant to be a downer. Consider it *"instruction through avoidance."* We all have moments when we are down on ourselves, or we doubt our abilities, or just lose some of our confidence. Some of us have these problems more often or to a greater extent.

Examine each of the following *"failure factors"* carefully. Determine if your personality exhibits any of the traits associated with them, and/or if your fears and doubts are fed by any of them. Some of these factors are fueled by the poor decisions people make and the ways they go about trying to avoid them. Be honest with yourself, as we're going to try to get past these things here and now, once and for all. I simply refuse to allow them to be factors preventing you from using the information in this book and building a successful and fulfilling business.

Lack of Confidence

You might have a lack of confidence in your knowledge, abilities, intelligence or social skills. Whatever your IQ, forget about it in relation to this book and the affiliate marketing concept. If you're reading this, you're fine...really! This isn't rocket science, just a process with specialized knowledge, and I'm going to give you that knowledge as you proceed.

Also, you're not going to be getting up in front of a camera or a room full of people and giving sales pitches. Your public speaking ability isn't important. Most of what you'll be doing is in front of your computer, so your people and social skills don't have to rise to the level of, say, a politician. Do computers scare you? So what if you're a one-finger typist! It may take you a bit longer to get things done, but it won't diminish your capability for success even one little bit.

Higher Education Deficit Disorder

This one plagues a lot of people. How many people do you know with college degrees who are toiling away as lower-level bank managers, or customer service representatives in retail stores, or feeling secure but underpaid in low-level jobs? Start paying attention to the successful people you know who don't have a college degree, and I think you'll see that it's many more than you would have guessed.

Your success in Internet affiliate marketing is NOT dependent on your education.

- Got a little college? – You can do it
- No college classes at all? – You can do it.
- G.E.D. instead of a high school diploma? – You can do it.
- Dropped out in 7th grade to become a football star? – You can do it.

The *"It Takes Money to Make Money"* Belief

If we wanted to start a retail brick-and-mortar store right now, we had better get a lot of cash together or apply for some kind of financing. After all, we would need:

- bricks and mortar
- land to build on
- money for a long lease
- money to stock the shelves
- money to market and advertise in ways that will generate walk-in trade
- insurance, utilities, and employee salaries

There's more, but you get the idea. All of that is true…BUT, we're not starting that type of business. We don't need to have the entire infrastructure in place BEFORE we open the doors and collect our first dollar. Thinking like this only acts as an obstacle in your path to success. I'll show you how to get started for little or no money, depending on how fast you want to roll out, and how much Internet knowledge and Web site savvy you already have. Even if you know nothing about building Web sites or blogging, the free resources I'll give you will allow you to have a fully functioning business up and running in just days.

Biting Off More than You Can Chew

This is taking on more challenges than you can overcome in the beginning. It ties in with the previous item, in that you can try to start up more of a business than your abilities, personal or financial, can support. It's the *"I need to be rich in a hurry"* attitude. In this book, you'll set the plan and tools to get rich if that's what you want, and if your motivation and desire are there to go after it.

But, for many of us, shooting for the stars from day one is a recipe for failure. The beauty of affiliate marketing is that we can begin to build a business that can feed its own growth to almost any level you can imagine; but it doesn't need to start out any more complex than you can handle right now. Don't threaten the ultimate outcome by demanding it from the start. I'll show you how to immediately realize income, feeding your motivation and enthusiasm. That will then feed your desire and abilities to go to the next level, and so on. You can get to almost any level of income you can imagine, but do it with a sustainable plan.

The *"I Can't Sell"* Dilemma

I really like this one, because it's the easiest obstacle to overcome. Who cares if you couldn't sell a bucket of water to a rich man in the desert? I'll introduce you to people who have realized their dreams in affiliate marketing—and some of them would have had a cardiac arrest if you had told them they had to pitch a product door-to-door.

This is another *"read my lips"* moment. Internet affiliate marketing is NOT SELLING a product or service directly to the consumer. We leave that to the vendor on their Web sites or at their toll-free customer sales numbers. What we do is to bring that customer to the POS *("**P**oint **O**f **S**ale")*, through our marketing sites on the Web. Yes, there is some pre-selling going on there, but it's certainly not face-to-face. If you aren't great at writing Web content that generates clicks and hits, I'll be giving you resources that will do it for you.

Get this failure factor out of your head. You can be a total hermit, with a speech impediment, and an aversion to any conversation over three words. It doesn't matter. When you finish this book, you'll be able to put together a Web presence that will drive consumers to vendors, and get paid hansomely in the process.

How Do You Say *"Play Nice?"*

This actually may not always be a failure factor, as there are people out there who are successful at making money by misleading or manipulating others. But in the long run, if your affiliate marketing is structured to generate income with *"slight of hand"* tactics, it is likely that you'll never be a real success. If for no other reason, complaints to your network or the vendor can get you banned or cost you affiliate relationships.

This is a short one. This business works because your entire team has one goal in the end…a happy customer. The vendor wants to keep the customer long-term or for repeat sales, your network wants to keep the vendor's business, and you want your payout for bringing in that happy customer. The very reason you add value is in your ability to bring new consumers to your vendors through your network. Always concentrate on that value and how to enhance it, and that will assure your success.

CHAPTER 3

Who Are You &
What Do You Want?

This is a fun chapter, as it's so satisfying for me to help people realize the opportunities available to them through affiliate marketing. Part of that satisfaction comes from being able to relate it to their current circumstances and encouraging them in the belief that this business fits their particular situation and meets their needs. Who would be a good candidate for a successful affiliate marketing business?

A Stay-at-Home-Mom or Dad

There are no confines or restrictions on the Internet and there are no limitations as to the number of prospects you can reach, regardless of where you happen to spend most of your day. Unlike a customer waiting at the door for you to open in the morning, affiliate marketing is open 24/7/365, whether you're feeding the kids or doing the laundry.

Yes, children do take up a lot of your time, but the Internet and your computer will wait for you. Even if you only happen to have half an hour now, and an hour tonight, your business will still be there waiting for you, without the pressures of stocking the shelves or opening on time. Stay-at-home-moms and dads are wonderful affiliate marketers!

A Full-Time Student

Talk about a perfect setup! I started my first online business when I was a full-time pre-med student. Earning $4,800 the first month, I'd say without hesitation that any student, grade school or college, can start and sustain an affiliate marketing business. Much the same as the stay-at-home parent, your available time is fragmented, but your business doesn't require certain hours of attendance. Jump right in…the water's fine.

A Salesperson on The Road

It's a whole new world out there technologically. The Internet is everywhere, from coffee shops to bookstores. It's almost impossible to find a hotel now that doesn't offer high speed Internet access in the room, much of it wireless. Many more have one or more computers in the lobby for the use of their guests.

Actually, the traveling sales or businessperson is an ideal candidate for affiliate marketing. If you've traveled for business, how much time have you spent idly waiting for something, whether it's boarding a flight or dead time in a hotel because the meeting is early tomorrow morning? Most airports now have free *WiFi* and some of their lounges offer computer access if you aren't carrying a laptop. New *"netbooks"* are selling for under $200, with full Internet wireless capability.

What do you consider productive use of your time, watching movie reruns in the hotel room, or setting up your new blog site to generate click-throughs for the latest *Netflix* offer? Did you know that *Netflix* pays you just for getting them a customer on a free trial? I'll have more on that later.

Office Worker at a Desk All Day

First, I'm not suggesting any activity on your boss's time, or that your employer wouldn't want. But if you have breaks during the day or a lunch-hour, and if your boss will let you stay late or come in early to work on the Web on your own time, you don't even need a computer at home.

Perhaps your job involves phone support or phone sales and requires periods of inactivity waiting for the phone to ring. Use your dead time to better your life by working on your online business. There are many tasks that can be done in short periods of time, and like I said before, your Web business will wait for you to show up, no schedule required.

A Business Owner

Perhaps you already own a business. It may be doing well, and you've got great employees who handle the load for you. Much of your day is spent just taking their questions, or making the occasional policy decision. The rest of the time you've been surfing, checking out your investments, or trading stocks online. Why not make a better investment in another business of your own, using this time productively in building a future that doesn't require sitting at that desk all day?

Let's not even get into a discussion about the hassles involved with management, employee issues, emergencies, tardy workers and no-shows on sale days. Your computer will never ask for a raise or a day off, nor will your Web business experience a competitor moving in across the street offering cheaper services.

What about the Blue Collar Worker?

No matter what color your collar is, what tools you carry, or the type of truck you drive, this method for financial success works. Even *"Larry the Cable Guy"* could excel at affiliate marketing, assuming there was a cleanup of language on his sites. The fact that you come home from work with paint or grease on your clothes is never going to be a factor in the success of your affiliate marketing business.

Some of our greatest success stories are from people who have worked most of their lives in the trades or with tools. They actually find it to be a delightful change from their usual routines and enjoy being able to work at a desk with a computer after dinner every night. Some have realized that their work with people every day, perhaps repairing their home or car, gives them a bit of insight into the regular consumer's habits and attitudes. This insight helps in their crafting of Web site offers that generate clicks.

Success Story # 1 – Dan M.

Dan M, a drywall finisher in his fifties, realized that his physically demanding job couldn't remain his primary source of income. Like many in this age group today, he knew that he didn't have enough money tucked away to retire, so he was looking for a way to generate income on the Internet in his off hours at home.

In searching the Web for opportunity, Dan turned up my Web site, and decided to use my program, systems, and materials. There wasn't any hesitation, with Dan setting out to learn my proven methods and put them to use for his own online business. He was motivated, and his enthusiasm increased when he generated affiliate marketing income in his first week! The great thing about Dan is that he could see the light at the end of the tunnel. He could see how affiliate marketing and the income he could generate from it would change his life forever.

Someone with Physical Limitations

Opportunity for those who find other types of work impossible is almost limitless with affiliate marketing. Computers work in bed as well as anywhere else. There is even much-improved voice recognition software out there that can cut the typing and keypad work down to almost nothing.

The fact that you can't jog in the park is unimportant. If you need a wheelchair to get around, it's not a problem. Don't let physical issues slow you down even a little in finishing this book and becoming a success in affiliate marketing. If you can find a way to get data into a computer, that's all you need.

Lost Your Job? No Computer? No Worries!

If this is your situation, don't be discouraged, as you have more to gain than almost everyone else reading this book. In even the smallest of towns, there is usually a library with a bank of computers for patrons to use. I've already stated that we can get you going for little or no money, so your employment status isn't a problem.

In fact, you've got more time than almost every other person mentioned in this chapter! You can have your business up in a matter of days if you apply the information I give you here. Who knows? You may even be reading this book in a library, with your future business computer in the same room.

Consider Yourself Included

I could write volumes about those who can make this happen for them. If I haven't hit your situation, then include yourself here by default. There are few reasons or situations that could keep someone from taking this book, following the plan, and becoming successful in affiliate marketing.

Requirements for this business are mostly motivation and a desire to make it work. The rest of the logistics simply involve a computer and the Internet. Both of those items are in abundant supply from coffee shops to libraries. Don't wait, don't doubt, and don't fear. Just read on, follow the plan I give you, use the tools I'll introduce to you, and take the results to the bank. Actually, most of the results will go to the bank on their own via direct deposit!

SECTION II
WHAT IS AFFILIATE MARKETING & WHY IS IT SUCCESSFUL?

CHAPTER 1
It's not Retail and it's Not Selling

Starting a Retail Brick and Mortar Business

If you've ever started a brand new retail business that relied on walk-in customers, you know that it's a huge undertaking, with a long list of time consuming and expensive things that must be done in order to be successful. Some of the expense comes right out of your pocket for weeks to months before you even open the doors for your first customer.

Facility Costs

Whether buying an existing building, leasing a space, or building from scratch, location is a big expense. A lease will require a first month, last month and security deposit up front in most cases and, with the space needing to be set up for business, you may be paying a couple of months of rent before the doors ever open.

Even if you're buying an existing building, you'll have mortgage payments to make before you open the doors, not to mention up front down payment money. Then there are all sorts of utility connection costs during the space setup and getting ready for customers.

There's also insurance, a significant cost, as it's not just on the building and contents, but also a hefty premium for liability with customers on the premises.

Inventory

A husband and wife purchased an existing business in a ski town in Colorado. First, they had the expense of buying the business *"blue sky"* or *"good will"* as we call it. That's the good name of the business, as well as the expected ongoing business from existing customers.

There was also the expense of purchasing existing inventory, mostly ladies clothing, western wear and jewelry. The first two items alone cost over $80,000. However, this couple didn't want to limit the business to current items, as it didn't generate enough income. They wanted to add custom boots and an inventory that allowed a customer to try on virtually any size between 3 AAAA and 17 EEEE in size and there were at least thirty different leathers and even more colors they wanted to offer. Their concept was to provide customers with the ability to find an exact fit, then choose style and leather for a custom order. Thus, their initial inventory was going to cost almost $30,000 more and that was with a new store discount!

In some industries, there is something called a *"floor plan inventory."* The manufacturer or supplier allows you to stock items and not pay for them until a sale is made. This is common in the retail appliance business however, you are paying interest on the value of the inventory.

You can see right away, that even before any closing costs, rent on the building or other startup costs, we're looking at an initial investment of $110,000 for simple acquisition fees. Add in the marketing kickoff, and this couple was set up to spend around $140,000 before their first customer walked through the door.

Employee Expense

Ask any business person what their biggest headache is, and they'll usually say it's employees. There are so many laws and costs involved in advertising for help, interviewing legally, forms and procedures, and determining and discussing wages. Along with wages come payroll taxes and workman's compensation insurance.

We haven't even touched on absenteeism, possible employee theft, and the liability that goes with having employees. This liability extends to on-the-job injuries, but also to employee and customer lawsuit issues. Employee turnover is an additional significant expense in a retail business.

Employee related expense is pure overhead when employees are there to handle order processing, complaints and item returns. There is sales commission cost associated with using phone or floor sales people as well. If you have a warehouse, you'll pay someone to receive and ship goods, which are additional overhead expenses that force you to adjust your pricing upwards, or your potential profits downwards.

The Startup & Operational Costs for Affiliate Marketing

Now, let's take a look at an entrepreneur following my instructions and plan, starting a brand new Internet affiliate marketing business. This entrepreneur is in exactly the same position as our ski town business couple, with a brand new business and nothing in place.

Facility Costs

Our new affiliate marketer has everything they need in a corner of their family room or a spare bedroom. It's a desk, computer and Internet access. There's no outflow of cash for rent, though they can get cash back from their taxes by deducting home office expenses. The same goes for utilities, no more cash out, but cash back from taxes. Of course I am not a tax lawyer, so obviously you should seek advice from one once you get started.

They're not inviting customers into their home, so there's no high dollar liability insurance. No extra facility costs are incurred to get the business up and running. At some point, you may believe that a home office will work better for you, but it isn't necessary, and will be your decision based on lifestyle factors rather than necessity.

Don't have a computer yet? No worries. We've already talked about using the neighborhood library. Or, if concentration is a problem at home, you can take a notebook computer to a quiet coffee shop. On the flip side, if you have children and other things that keep you home-bound, then affiliate marketing on your home computer is just right for you.

Inventory

What inventory? Through affiliate marketing, you bring customers to companies who handle the inventory, and they pay you well for doing it. You keep absolutely no inventory for re-sale. You might need some computer paper, but that's $4.50 a ream at *Walmart*. Virtually everything you're about to do is going to be implemented on the Internet.

Let *Netflix*, *Best Buy* and others keep millions of dollars in inventory in multiple warehouses while you get to participate in their profits as they pay for the facility, inventory, insurance and other overhead costs.

Employee Expense

Again, what employees? You alone can do everything needed to get your affiliate marketing business going. And once you've set it up, it is mostly self-sustaining. No salaries, insurance, payroll taxes or other employee-related costs will be in your budget.

Another benefit is that your livelihood is completely dependent on your motivation, knowledge, desire and performance. Your income will not suffer due to employee neglect or indifference. You won't have emergency situations when a floor employee doesn't show up for work after you've spent thousands advertising a huge sale.

You will not need a staff to handle sales, complaints, or returns–there aren't going to be any. A wonderful benefit of affiliate marketing is that your money is made by getting the customer to the retailer, supplier or information provider. They manage the Web site and/or phone sales, handle deliveries, as well as complaints and returns. You've long since collected your money.

Let's Talk Competition in the Marketplace

Retail Brick and Mortar

We all know that two ice cream parlors on the same block can be a problem, but there are other considerations as well. If you're still managing to eke out a living as a pharmacy or local hardware store, it's likely that *Walmart* hasn't placed a store too close to you yet. A small retail business is at great risk from big box stores. You can't blame the customer who can buy the same item for 20% less from the big box vendor.

The start-up and operational costs we've already discussed make it a huge risk to get into a retail brick and mortar business today. The overhead required for day-to-day operation makes your business vulnerable to any new local competitor with a better idea, or lower overhead costs. Or maybe they just don't know their costs, and their lower prices will eventually put them out of business. But will they go first, or will you?

eBay and Other Online Marketplaces

What if you found a resource, say, for example, a business in bankruptcy, with large inventories of items you think you can sell? First, you'll need to buy them, so we're back to the inventory dilemma. There's an upfront investment, and what if they don't sell? Let's say that you're confident that these items are in demand on *eBay*. You already have your little store set up, and you take *PayPal* and credit cards. Now, let's choose a couple of items, and see how searches on *eBay* look:

- *"Pocket watch"* – 18,639 results. Now, you could have made a heck of a deal on a thousand pocket watches, but it looks like there are quite a few others out there with the same idea.
- *"Used cell phone"* with 19,502 results, and "unlocked cell phone" with 36,314 results. Wow, I'm really looking forward to top dollar for those 1500 cell phones I just invested in.

The problem is that these *eBay* sellers aren't just beating each other's brains out; they are in continual competition with retailers selling the same brand new items. Retailers, like *Best Buy*, have many more resources for deep discount buying than the little guy selling on *eBay*. It's becoming clear that the micro-business today must have an edge to be successful; but, don't despair, because I'm going to show you how to:

- Work without facility costs
- Run your business without overhead for utilities, insurance and salaries
- Never handle merchandise or take inventory risk
- Never deal with complaints or returns
- Make your money getting paid by retailers competing against each other
- In fact, you can have them compete for your business!

Success Story # 2 – Halie

Halie writes: *"I am a stay at home mother of two boys. I had been looking for something I could do from home and bring in some extra income. I came across Anthony Morrison's system and followed it step-by-step. In my first month, I made around $360. The next month it jumped to $1,500, then $2,300, and it just keeps growing.*

I didn't have to go out and find other books, systems or tools. I just use exactly what Anthony teaches, and it works. The key to my success was the clear instructions, which create an income system that anyone can duplicate. Every month brings new excitement, as I watch the income increase, and look forward to the same next month.

Anthony's system has worked for me and it can work for you. All you have to do is to put in a little time and effort. Success is up to you. Just follow Anthony's system and you will succeed like I have."

What is Affiliate Marketing & How Does it Work?

The Big Picture

It helps most people to visualize the big picture before they drill down to specifics and details, so let's look at that now. Affiliate marketing involves three major entities, each an independent portion of the whole:

1. A retailer, wholesaler or service vendor who wants to generate more customers and business via their Web site.
2. An affiliate network that contracts with these businesses to bring them customers.
3. Affiliate marketers then set up their Internet marketing to deliver these customers through the affiliate network to the vendor.

Now, the retailer knows that they can spend a fortune to do their own online marketing, but along with that expense is the overhead of maintaining many Web sites and having to monitor their results. They approach an affiliate network, offering them compensation based on their ability to deliver customers. The affiliate network does just what their name implies, building a network of affiliate marketers who are each building sites and blogs to market the products and services the vendors have placed with the network.

Another consideration the brick and mortar retailers take into account is their cost of sales in the physical stores. There they have the facility costs, as well as sales commissions and employee salaries. So, if they can sell the same item to an Internet customer, they have some of these cost savings to pay out to affiliates to get the customer to their site.

We know what the retailer has to gain, and that they get their income from the end customer transaction. But how does the rest of the process work, and how are affiliates and their networks compensated? The beauty of affiliate marketing is that everyone wins when the Internet consumer does what we want.

1. The consumer locates an enticing offer or link at an affiliate marketing site.
2. They click on it, ending up at the retailer's site, but with a tracking code that shows where they came from.
3. This code indicates the affiliate marketer and their network.
4. The retailer has contracted to pay the network a set amount or percentage for each conversion.
5. The affiliate network takes a small commission off the top, paying the agreed amount (or *"payout"*) to the affiliate marketer.

This is a really democratic system, as there are no conflicts of interest. Everybody involved wins, even the consumer, as they end up with the product, service, or free trial they want. The affiliate marketer (you when you finish this book) isn't the bottom of the chain, they're the beginning. Without our efforts placed into building excellent Web sites and blogs, search engine strategies to get the consumers to them, and the right content to get that click, nobody wins.

When we succeed, our affiliate network gets paid as well, so they want to help us in any way possible to succeed in developing our sites, blogs and other marketing venues. They are competing among each other for the business of the vendors and retailers, as well as higher payouts from them based on their performance but, their performance is dependent on ours.

Even better, let's look at the whole competition piece again. Remember, there are many competitors for every item on *eBay*. Also, remember that the retailers, even the major chains, all have competitors. The cell phone carriers are an excellent example of extreme competition. Electronics retailers, like *Best Buy* are also in fierce competition, as are booksellers like *Amazon* and *Borders*. As affiliate marketers, we have the enviable position of getting paid no matter who wins.

Yes, our networks are sending business to these competitors, and we're the vehicle for it. So you can have a really great blog about digital cameras, maybe a review site, and when you do an excellent job of generating traffic to your site, there may be offers there from multiple camera vendors and major electronics chains. You won't care who gets the business, as you'll get paid anyway. Whenever they click, buy, or take the desired action, there's a payday in it for you and your network.

An *iPhone* App Store Example

Let's say that there is a group of cool programmers out there who have the *iPhone* figured out, and they have developed a group of really great applications for it. They plan on selling several to any one business subscriber, as they are primarily designed to help them do a better job with appointments, business management, and contact management for sales. There is even an app for custom sales order forms. Maybe they've set their price at $29.95 for each application. They approach multiple affiliate networks with their plan, and set up accounts. There are three ways in which they can approach this, and they'll be likely to try variations of all three to see what works best:

1. Straight sale offers, with the affiliate marketer (perhaps a business blogger) linking to a specific application for contact management. If the consumer buys, the network gets $x or x% of the sale amount. This could be a major portion of the whole sale, with the advertiser hoping to then follow up with offers of their other apps, but only paying once for this customer. The network takes their cut off the top, giving the major portion of the payment to the affiliate that sent the buyer.

2. The link from the affiliate blogger site is to a free trial of one of their applications. A sale isn't certain, but this advertiser is pretty confident in their application, and believes that the free trial will result in a conversion to a purchase, plus future purchases of the

other apps in the suite of products, as they all interact. In this case, the dollar amount to the network may be smaller, but it's going to result in more conversions, as the consumer doesn't have to spend any money.

3. Generally, if the product costs are higher, they can offer a payment just for the lead, meaning they'll pay if the consumer comes from your affiliate link to their site and just submits a small amount of information like their name and E-mail address. This will usually result in the highest conversion rate, but the payouts will be the smallest.

Let's stay with this example a little longer. This advertiser probably approached several networks, and will likely end up working with more than one. As an affiliate marketer, you are likely to find them on the list of advertisers of more than one of the networks with which you work. There was negotiation on their end with the networks. Some would have demonstrated the probability that they would generate more business for the advertiser, and thus negotiated a higher overall payout.

You find this advertiser on a couple of your networks. Your decision as to which offer you'll place on your sites and market will be based on which will result in the highest payout to you. One network may be keeping a higher portion for their income, leaving less for you, even though both are receiving the same from the advertiser. That's assuming other factors are equal, such as incentives or the tools you have on a network. If one has super *iPhone* ad apps, it may tip the scales their way with a lower payout for this particular offering. Or, you could create multiple marketing pieces and do them both as a test, using the results to kill one and stay with the other.

You'll find that many advertisers will consistently run very different offers, often with very different payout amounts and methods. It isn't always a test, in that some may work best with certain consumer demographic groups. They may retain a free trial offer, paying you less, but converting well with consumers who are resistant to buying something they can't try first. Then, they may keep an ongoing offer out there for a straight purchase, maybe with a new customer discount. This one is for the early adopter, or consumer who has no problem spending money if they like the ad copy.

Introduction to the Affiliate Networks

We're talking about affiliate networks, so this is a good time to introduce you to some of the largest. It's not so that you can select one or two. You're going to want to join every network you can locate. Why? First, some networks will have exclusive arrangements with vendors, so you'll only get access to those if you are a member of that network. Then, there's comparing their payment schedules, methods, and most important, the payouts they offer. Some networks also offer incentive programs, with points that you accumulate toward all kinds of products, services and more. We'll talk more about payouts and the different forms they take a little later.

Definitions You Will Need to Know

Affiliate Manager – As we'll be mentioning which networks offer affiliate managers, let's define what an affiliate manager is and their role in your success. Many networks have online sign up: you set yourself up, learn their tools and interface, and then use their tools to place the affiliate links on your sites.

Other networks have real people in managerial positions to help you succeed and motivate you along the way. Remember that the network wins when you win, and networks who have decided to use affiliate managers have decided that by using them they increase the success of their affiliates, thus raising everybody's income. So, your success is important to your affiliate manager, as they receive bonuses when their group of affiliates does well.

Think of your affiliate manager as a coach who keeps their job and prospers by building a great team, training them well, and helping them to win in the marketplace. Part of the team-building is getting the best performing affiliates on the team. Later on, we'll talk about how you can use this for your benefit, negotiating higher payouts for you if they want you on their team.

CPL (*"Cost Per Lead"*) – You are paid when your link brings a potential customer to the vendor. This is whether they purchase now or in the future. They are paying you to bring them a lead, and they take on the task of selling that lead once delivered by you.

Because a purchase isn't required, you will generally see higher conversion rates with CPL. You'll get more leads to the vendor, but the payout for each is lower, as they aren't sure of any income from the lead. However, the vendor can alter your return based on the method they use to handle the lead once they click through to the site from your affiliate link.

A lead typically is counted only after the customer fills out a form on the advertiser's landing page. The size of the form, and how much information it requires can make a big difference in whether the customer completes and submits it. If they don't fill out the form, no lead for affiliate payment is processed.

A *"long form lead"* is one name for a form that requires a great deal of information from the customer. They can require as much as:

- Name
- E-mail address
- Phone number
- Household income
- Think of what you don't want to tell them, and it may be what they want to know

These long forms convert to paid leads at a much lower percentage, as the customer must fill in so much information that they balk, and leave the site at a much higher rate. Though the payout on these leads may be higher than with other types of lead offers, the conversion rate can be low enough to completely wipe out any payout advantage.

"Short form leads" are those that usually require only the customer's name and E-mail address. The advertiser is far more likely to get the form submitted, but they experience a lower ultimate conversion rate, as the easier form encourages less serious inquiries. Regardless, you will realize a greater conversion rate to a paid lead. The trade-off is lower payouts.

I'm teaching you what to look for when comparing affiliate networks, advertisers, offers and payouts. This comparison of lead form type and associated payouts can increase your dollar return significantly just by comparing the expected conversion rate projections of two different offers for the same item or service. There are retailers out there that change the entire layout of store aisles at great expense, just to get half of a percent more in purchases. You only need to choose the right advertiser and best offer to do far better.

CPA ("Cost per Action") – CPA requires consumer participation. They aren't just delivered to the vendor for sales activity on that site hoping to convert the lead, the consumer is required to take some action. It could be a purchase, but it could also require the consumer to sign up for a free trial. Either is defined as an *"action,"* and means an immediate sale, and/or indicates that there is a very good chance that they'll sign up from a free trial.

Netflix is a great example. They experience a high conversion rate from their free trials, and also from promotions offering very low cost introductory month fees; however, they're willing to pay you as an affiliate an amount of money that puts them in the hole for a few months. *Netflix* has documented results that indicate they will retain the majority of these customers long-term.

Carefully examine CPA offers, as it is important to understand what is required from the customer in order for you to get paid. A straight forward free trial with no strings attached is great, however, many free trial offers require consumers to enter valid credit card information and pay an activation fee. This fee, though it may be small, is a deterrent to customer sign up, and can greatly reduce conversion rates. If they don't sign up, your effort has been wasted because you won't get paid.

Though *Netflix* requires an activation fee for free trial offers, they have purposely made that fee very low. This increases their conversion rate dramatically. So, when you're comparing CPA offers and payouts, always consider and compare:

- Is the same advertiser or product/service offered via CPL?
- Would CPL work better for you?
- If CPA–Is credit card information required?
- Is an activation fee charged?
- How much is the activation fee?

You'll experience lower conversion rates as an affiliate with CPA, but generally the payout is higher per conversion. Over time, you'll gain experience in relating CPL and CPA to the offer and the product or service and gain an understanding about the potential benefits of your efforts.

% Percent of Sale – This is like a floor sales person's commission. When you bring a consumer to a vendor's site and offer, and they take the plunge and buy, you get a stated percentage of the sale amount. Of course, it's easy to see what you're going to make, and that can mean quite a bit of money for you if it's a high dollar purchase. Conversion rates are lower, but individual payouts can be quite nice with percent of sale.

I always suggest that you take a good look at the advertiser's Web site before running a % of sale offer. How they lay out their site, the information they provide, their sales approach, and their prices are all important to conversion. If you were interested in the product, would you be able to find it on their Web site?

If you like the site and how it accommodates the customer, then look at the price of the offer in relation to the percentage you receive if your visitor translates into an actual sale. A $3.00 item that pays you 15% isn't going to make you much money, while a $500 item that pays the same 15% may make this an offer you want to promote.

The Networks

Let's take a brief look at a few major affiliate networks now. They are listed in no particular order.

www.linkshare.com
This is a large network, but not very personalized. You do not have access to affiliate managers with this network. A scroll window on their home page shows vendor clients, including *AT&T, Macy's, Apple, iTunes, Office Depot* and *TigerDirect*.

www.copeac.com
A quote from their home page tells their story: *"It's no surprise why COPEAC is the fastest growing affiliate network. Top converting offers, weekly payouts, dedicated affiliate managers, creative development, and much more make COPEAC the network of choice for over 30K affiliates."* This network offers affiliate managers and incentive points.

www.cxdigital.com
This is another excellent network that offers affiliate managers and incentive points programs. From their home page: *"The CX Digital Media Affiliate Network is a leader in performance based online marketing featuring CPA advertising (Cost Per Action)."* A quick look at their site today showed an announcement that new members could qualify for a $750 performance bonus. That's an example of creating an incentive for affiliate performance right from the start.

www.neverblue.com

This network gives you your own affiliate manager, and their home page scroll shows clients like *Gamefly, eHarmony, CellFish, FlyCell, Perfect Match* and more. What they say: *"As a premier lead generation network, Neverblue values strong affiliates, because they're what make us better! Join Neverblue and experience a sophisticated, globally connected affiliate network that helps you focus on results!"*

www.cj.com

Commission Junction is a very large network, with hundreds of offers, but no affiliate managers. Their system even allows the creation of links to product groups, such as the search results page for "all-in-one printers" on one major retail site.

www.icommissions.com

This network focuses mainly on credit related offers. They have very good affiliate support and affiliate managers. Their offers concentrate in the areas of credit cards, pre-paid cards, auto loans, and personal loans.

www.hydranetwork.com

A large network that assigns an affiliate manager to you! From their home page: *"Hydra's affiliate network offers the most campaigns, most exclusives, most personalized service, and best conversions to help you make more money. Plus, we'll beat any payout and always pay on time!"* We'll talk about network competition for your business with higher payouts later.

www.expressrevenue.com

This is a smaller network, but does make affiliate managers available to you. What they say: *"Here at Express Revenue, we pledge to our affiliates exactly what is explicitly stated in our name. Through the integration of a very user friendly and navigable Web site, always available customer support, and a unique All-In-One approach, Express Revenue makes it possible for your marketing business to gain higher amounts of revenue and more quality leads than what you could have previously imagined!"*

www.pepperjamnetwork.com

This is a pretty large network, and many of their offers are percent of sale. You have access to an affiliate manager as well. Their *"Featured Advertisers"* page lists partners including *NetShops, FlyCell, DentalPlans.com, SinglesNet.com,* and *LifeLock.*

www.azoogle.com
This large network advertises that they focus on CPA offers, and that they have many exclusives you won't get in other networks. They have a good incentive rewards program, and they offer affiliate managers.

www.clickbank.com
This network doesn't offer affiliate managers, and specializes mainly in digital products for online delivery. *E-Books* are big on this network.

I want you to get through this entire book before you start signing up for these networks, but once you've completed the book, sign up for ALL of them. Why? Because you will end up working with several, but you won't know which networks are best for you until you compare them based on:

- Their advertisers and products and how those match your interests and knowledge strengths
- Whether they offer affiliate managers, and how you'll gain from this with its cost to you in payouts
- Incentive and points programs
- The frequency and schedule of their payouts
- Most of all, compare their payouts for the very same products and advertisers

It's ALL Negotiable

You noticed in the network list that a few of them make a point of mentioning *"top payouts."* Others mention *"matching payouts"* on their sites. One even features bonuses for new affiliates. This tells you that there is competition for your business. Don't think that just because you're new to this that you must settle for whatever they offer you in terms of payouts. Evaluate affiliate networks based on all of the factors we have discussed, and how these factors will eventually translate into dollars in your pocket.

Structure and Demographics

First, take a look at a networks' list of advertisers. Who do they serve, and who do they feature on their site? As I mentioned above, one particular network primarily handles digital products, which means there are many smaller or unknown vendors selling reports and *e-Books*. That doesn't necessarily mean it's a deal killer for you, as many of these vendors are paying more than 50% of sale as a commission. There could be good money in it, especially if you have knowledge in an area that could both facilitate your blog or Web site building and enable you to adapt an authoritative tone that will ultimately help you deliver those clicks to the vendors.

Does the network seem to have a higher percentage of CPL, CPA or % of Sale? In our definitions, I touched on the differences and how this impacts the total dollars you'll realize. Each has pluses and minuses, and the method has a lot to do with the product or service, and the amount of effort and money that the consumer must invest before you see a return.

Others may specialize in reaching a specific demographic attracted to sites that offer things such as gaming, music, ring tones, fun *iPhone* apps or other digital, hardware and software products that appeal to a younger audience. They have money to spend, and this audience is all over the Web.

The larger networks tend to represent advertisers with products and services that appeal to almost everyone. You'll be building blogs and Web sites with content designed to inspire a site visitor to read all of the content and then click on an affiliate link. No click, no income. So, you may want to consider using products and services that you have some knowledge of from the start. This will help you get that content up online faster. However, if you have a budget and resources, I'll show you later how you can hire inexpensive writers to create content for you and direct you to their Web sites. Many writers will even post their availability to provide services in your blogs.

Tools They Offer

Some networks are stronger in the area of tools availabe to you for your marketing efforts. Some have *iPhone* apps, special *Google* tools, and other features that make it faster for you to promote their advertisers. Maybe the tools provide a flashier set of buttons or better displays to catch your site visitor's attention.

What if you could get a small piece of code to place on your Web site that would display all of an advertiser's offers instantly, and change when the offers change? This is called a *"feed,"* and networks that work with their advertisers to develop these feeds should be higher on your list of preferences. After all, if you can display twenty offers in the same amount of time it would take you to display one, you will be saving time and time is money.

These tools aren't the most important things in your network selection decisions, but saving time or catching the eye of more visitors is part of increasing your productivity and your income. Sometimes, button designs can double your click-through rate.

Network Reputation

Every business that has longevity develops a reputation among its customers, present and past. As an affiliate marketer you are both a supplier to and customer of the networks. You deliver clicks and revenue, and it's in their best interests to serve you well in order to keep you doing just that.

Just a couple of years ago, it was more difficult to get an overall perception of an affiliate networks reputation. The old ways of doing research still work, and you can simply ask other affiliate marketers about their experiences as you get to know them. Today, it's a whole new world out there, with social and business networks like *Twitter* and *LinkedIn* having a strong presence on the Internet. *LinkedIn* is primarily a business oriented site, with a big *"Questions and Answers"* feature.

A *LinkedIn* member with expertise in a specific field, and a desire to market themselves, can build a network by answering questions related to their field within the site. In fact, a search on *LinkedIn* yields several hundred questions with the keywords *"affiliate network."* *LinkedIn* is free to join and you have an opportunity to ask a certain number of questions, so you can inquire about a network and see who responds with their experience.

Now *Twitter* is really an interesting resource. I just did a *Twitter* search on the names of several affiliate networks, and there were plenty of tweets about each of them. Of course, there were the expected marketing posts, but there were also testimonials and a complaint or two as well. Many businesses have seized the opportunity presented on *Twitter* as a way to handle their customers' questions or problems efficiently. Give it a try.

Pay Schedules & Methods

We'll talk about payout amounts later; let's talk about schedules. How often does the network pay out, monthly, quarterly, or weekly? Many networks have payment thresholds that don't pay out until a specific amount is actually due to you. This is usually not a problem once you get going, but it can create delays in your quest to earn much needed seed money if you happen to be new and the payout threshold is high. The same situation can occur if the network has other rules that delay payout.

Clickbank is an example of rules delaying payouts. As much of their product is digital, with a huge number of *eBooks* by unknown authors, experts and gurus, there is a concern about returns and complaints about the value of the product received. *Clickbank* has payout rules that delays payment to allow for returns. There are also restrictions that require a certain number of transactions, and the same for requiring different payment methods to season an account.

It's not that there aren't good reasons for some of these restrictions; but only you can determine if they would result in delayed payouts that are unacceptable for your business. Particularly if the payout levels are comparable, but one network pays out faster and with fewer restrictions, you'll know which way to go.

Also consider *how* are you paid. It isn't the norm, but there are still networks that mail paper checks. This just adds another delay to the process, and a trip to the bank to deposit the check. If it's a great network, with high payouts, it's a minor inconvenience. But networks that deposit electronically, directly into your bank account, mean less hassle for you and faster access to that money. Many will pay you through *PayPal* as well. If payouts and other factors are the same, I would choose the one that gets the money directly into my account fastest. Make sure that you are aware of any fees associated with getting your money to you as well. If they charge you for direct deposit, factor that into the next discussion of payouts and negotiate the best payouts possible.

Payouts – What is Offered & the Negotiation

Of course, high on your list of comparisons of affiliate networks is their payout amounts. What they offer to a new affiliate is based on a number of factors:

- What they have negotiated with their vendor advertiser
- Their expense of doing business, including commissions for their affiliate managers (if they have them).
- Their affiliate base and performance – those with huge numbers of productive affiliates will be able to take a smaller percentage and still remain quite profitable.

That last item is really important, and something that you must keep in mind when you are dealing with your affiliate manager. We've already talked about the greatest value of our team; that everybody wins if the affiliate marketer wins. They want you to be successful, because increases in your income mean increases in theirs. This includes your affiliate manager. Their focus is on motivating you, and helping you to achieve the highest income possible. They are paid based on their success in this respect, and they can receive bonuses when their affiliate group performs well for the network.

When an affiliate has been with a network for a while, and their performance has been excellent, they will be courted with incentives and higher payouts. Many of these networks have point systems that reward their affiliates with everything from *iPods* to sports cars. Of course, your goal is to be one of those affiliates, and getting your income up is right at the top of your list. But why would you wait for higher payouts when you don't have to?

Remember, networks must have a payout system that has built-in room for this ratcheting up of compensation for high performers. Their standard offers on the site for new affiliates, whether new to the game or just to that network, are at the lowest level they believe they can set and still attract a new affiliate. Your job, even if you're brand new to this game, is to convince the affiliate manager that you're a prize catch, and worth initial payouts higher than they are offering.

You're ready to enter into this payout negotiation when you've joined multiple networks and carefully compared their payouts. Chart them on a spreadsheet by type of advertiser, CPL, CPA and % of Sale. It's important that you have a firm grasp of the actual dollar amount that would hit your account in a specific comparison action.

Example: You find that most of the networks are working with *Netflix*, and you chart out their payouts offered to a new affiliate on their site. Then you do the same for other advertiser types that are represented by the networks, such as electronics retailers, etc.

Now you're ready to negotiate with the affiliate manager with a network you like. The fact that you're new to the network is obvious, but there need be no mention of the fact that you're new to this game. I'm going to give you three approaches to the negotiation.

THREE KILLER STRATEGIES FOR HIGHER PAYOUTS

1. **The Question & the Offer** – If you approach the affiliate manager with a requirement for higher payouts than their usual standard offer, it's likely that you'll be asked *"What do you need?"* Since you don't know, and don't want to tell them this, come back with, *"Why don't you come back to me with a more competitive structure so that I can compare it to what I've been offered by other networks?"* You haven't said you have a better offer, you've merely implied it. And the other implication is that you'll go elsewhere if this network's offer isn't high enough. What you're doing here is putting the ball into the affiliate manager's court. They don't know how profitable an affiliate you will be, but they'll never know if they lose you at the start. Not wanting to insult you with a lower payout than you might have been offered elsewhere, they will typically come back to you with an offer that's almost at the top of their payout range. The fact that you asked for their best offer indicates that you're not the "newbie" who takes what's offered or asks lamely, *"Can't you do better?"* They believe that you "know the ropes," and they'll come back near *to* or *at* their best offer.

   OR

2. **The Give & Takeaway Approach** – Actually run a real offer on your site for a few days, get good results and then pull the offer. Show the results to the affiliate manager and tell him or her that you are going to have to take it to another network offering a better payout. Keep in mind that he or she knows that all you have to do is to change the link on your site to make this happen. Always remember that fact. The bulk of your work is in setting up Web sites, blogs and online marketing materials. There is text to write and links or buttons to put into the marketing media. To change the link to a different network and offer is a couple of minutes for you. But that couple of minutes cuts off the revenue for one network and delivers it to another. An example would be a history of your account pulling in five conversions of *Netflix* offers every day. This is consistent,

and the affiliate network is accustomed to these five deals every day from your efforts. Threatening to take them to another network will usually result in a quick increase in your payout, and an increase in your payout percentage is far better than losing 100% of the income.

OR

3. **The $100k Play –** Remember, you're not new to the game for this discussion, just new to this network. Be confident, and let the affiliate manager believe that you have the knowledge and experience to do precisely what you tell them you plan to do. I always start off by telling my affiliate manager exactly what I plan to do such as: *"I've put the mechanism in place, and would like to do $100k in the next 30 days. But I'm going to need a better payout to do it with this network, as I have better offers from others."* With this approach you will most likely get your affiliate manager so excited that they will give you the highest possible payouts instantly. All they can think about is that $100k number you talked about on the phone. They instantly forget about trying to keep big margins on the offer payouts because they are excited about the volume of business you could bring to the network. Remember, affiliate managers typically earn a commission, and they are evaluated based on the success rate of their affiliates. They will do almost anything to get an affiliate that can generate $100k a month, and as long as you really do plan on trying to reach that goal, it works out for both you and the affiliate manager.

Here's the common thread in these three strategies: you get a better deal or you take your business elsewhere. If you really think about it, their risk is only a few bucks at the beginning to see if you're really going to be a profit generator for them. The risk is that they'll send away a strong affiliate who they would have given the better payout deal to anyway in a month or so.

Now let's look at this negotiation from another perspective. You have completed this book, and you're absolutely certain that you have the knowledge and tools to be a major affiliate producer for any networks with which you choose to work. You're not coming to these affiliate managers with your hat in your hand asking for a handout. You are actually offering them the opportunity to make a decision early in your relationship that will bring in profits for them down the road. You want to offer them your future performance, but you're not the normal affiliate, and you want to be compensated at a rate above average as well.

Schmooze With Your Affiliate Manager for Success

I've just given you detailed information about how to manipulate your af-filiate manager into giving you higher payouts, and it works. Now, it may sound contradictory to tell you to schmooze with your affiliate manager, and become their friend if you can. Your affiliate manager is the person at the network who fights for your business, and relies on your performance for their income and job security. Knowing this, it would seem that you have the upper hand, and just need to negotiate the best payouts and bring in the business. Many successful affiliates work just this way, never building a deeper relationship with their affiliate manager.

They may be successful, but these affiliates do not realize that there is greater success and more fun to be had if their affiliate manager likes them on a personal level. This business isn't all payout numbers and clicks. The money that funds the network and our business comes from those clicks, but there is a budget at most networks for affiliate perks and other benefits that some affiliates never learn about. Let's look at specific rea-sons to build a better and more personal relationship with your affiliate manager.

1. The most obvious is that they'll fight even harder to maximize your payouts if they like you. It's just human nature. Getting past the numbers, relationships do contribute to your income in affiliate marketing.
2. For a variety of reasons, either from the advertiser's or the network's perspective, some offers are exclusive, only given to a select group of affiliates. What if you could promote an offer that only 10 other af-filiates in the world were promoting as well? That's thousands fewer competitors than the offers available to the entire network. How much would your income increase if your competition was reduced by 99%? With many of these exclusive offers directly controlled by the affiliate managers, they will be deciding which affiliates make this very short and profitable promotion list. Building a good relationship with your affiliate manager could make the difference between competing with the masses, and increasing your profits with offers limited to a select few chosen affiliates.

Of course when I started in the affiliate marketing business, this book didn't exist. I was new to the business, with little knowledge of its work-ings, and nobody to teach me. In learning everything on my own, I gained a great deal of experience quickly, but it was also costly in many ways. In this book, I'm short-circuiting your learning curve, cutting out all of my mistakes, taking you at warp speed to a successful affiliate marketing business. An example of how the information in this book can jump-start your business is Justin K.

Success Story #3 – Justin K.

Starting my affiliate marketing business in college, the only goal then was to help to support my family after my father's fortune was lost in the WorldCom collapse. Affiliate marketing was one of the ways that I generated money to continue my education and to help my family through our crisis. The motivation was intense, and I quickly reached an income of several thousand dollars a month. When this happened, people began to notice, one of them my good friend Justin.

Justin and I were in college together, and the very best of friends. I really respected Justin, primarily because of who he was as a person. He was an all-around great guy. He would do anything for anyone at any time. Our friendship was such that he was always at my dorm room studying, as we were both trying to get into medical school. Being together so much, Justin quickly noticed that I was on my computer a lot checking money coming in from my business. A smart guy, he realized that it was a really amazing income for a college kid running a business between classes.

Justin was preparing for marriage and studying to get into optometry school. The responsibilities of marriage at this stage changed his focus a bit to income generation, and he wanted a fallback position in case he didn't get into optometry school. Justin was also working at his Dad's suit store, but that income wasn't going to take care of his household. He asked if I would teach him to do what I was doing, and of course I said I would. I was thrilled to help him out. We sat down together, and I taught him everything I knew to that point, and how it was generating those thousands of dollars every month.

> *There was no hesitation on Justin's part in getting started and setting up his affiliate marketing business. I introduced him to my affiliate manager, and he was soon generating several thousand dollars a month as well. Of course this made my affiliate manager quite happy. Using the techniques and strategies I taught him, at the time I'm writing this book, Justin has generated over $1,000,000.00 in affiliate marketing income! He's now generating an income that neither of us ever dreamed was possible in that college dorm room.*

Justin, using this affiliate marketing income, was able to pay cash for a new home for him and his wife. Under 30 years old, Justin will never have to worry about paying a mortgage, or what would happen if he couldn't. Foreclosure isn't a word that concerns him. Changing a life is what this book is all about. You can change your life with affiliate marketing. All you need to get started is the wisdom, knowledge, and direction that I'm going to give you in this book. You can create your own success story, just like the one's you'll be reading here.

Anyway, back to Justin, and the point of this story about schmoozing with your affiliate manager. That's a concept I hadn't taught Justin early on, as I really wasn't doing it much myself. I believed I had a good relationship with my affiliate manager. After all, I brought Justin to him, didn't I? I even took a trip to his office to meet him personally, so we could both put a face with the name. I even attended a concert with him. The fact that I wasn't doing enough was brought home to me when he offered an exclusive marketing opportunity to Justin, not me. This baffled me because:

1. I was doing more revenue with the network than Justin was at that time, so making more money for my affiliate manager.
2. I brought Justin to the network, helping my affiliate manager even more.
3. I had been with the network much longer than Justin

So, I'm sitting there wondering what in the world was going on. Everything I knew indicated to me that I should have gotten that exclusive offer before Justin. Yet, my greater volume and longer term with the network didn't make it happen. The fact that my efforts resulted in more income to the affiliate manager made no difference. Justin was happily marketing the exclusive offer and raking in the profits.

After I finished stewing about it, I took to heart something that you have the advantage of learning right now: business isn't always about volume and money. People do business, and relationships are a part of it. You can make millions in affiliate marketing, creating comfortable commissions for your affiliate manager, but still not get perks and exclusive offers, just because there isn't a personal relationship with your affiliate manager. It doesn't even have to be that they don't like you. They just have to like someone else better, and the reasons may be unrelated to the income they bring in.

I suggest a phone conversation with your affiliate manager at least once every other day, just to get to know them better. Ask about their life, family, friends and hobbies. All of the pleasantries you extend to your friends and some of those for your family should be part of this relationship. Send them birthday and Christmas cards. Send them a link to a great Web site about their hobby or favorite pastime. This may all sound silly to you, but you never know what little thing you do will set you apart in the mind of your affiliate manager. When the next exclusive offer comes around, it may be that one little thing that will put a whole lot of dollars in your pocket.

Justin's success story is not just about taking what I taught him and applying it successfully. It was about taking what I taught him to the next level. It's about taking action with an idea, even if you didn't learn it in this book. I'm giving you every tool I have for successful affiliate marketing, but don't discount any new idea that you may have. Give it a try.

Bringing it all Together

I've given you the reasons why affiliate marketing is so lucrative for the few who really understand it and apply their knowledge with a plan, the right tools and the motivation to succeed in these last two chapters. This book is where you're getting the knowledge, tools, and confidence to realize any income goal you have with affiliate marketing.

We've learned that the costs to get into this business are tiny compared to getting into almost any retail business. We've also learned that the competition is fierce at the advertiser level. You get to let advertising fight for the business, while you can link out to all of them, taking the income from the one who has the best offer at the moment. You don't care which one, you are just delivering their customer.

I've explained how you can get the help you need from your networks and affiliate managers. They will only succeed if you do. They want you to be out there making as much money as you can, as their prosperity is based on yours. Knowing that you have clout, and that you are capable of manipulating and maneuvering the best payout deal possible, will better prepare you to negotiate with your affiliate managers for better deals, including great incentive programs. I gave you three specific approaches to your payout negotiations.

We now have a basic understanding of CPA, CPL and % of Sale. I've also given you a foundation in how each influences payout, with the product and offer factored into the equation. We know that generally a free trial will result in more conversions, as it doesn't require money for the action. This means a lower dollar payout, but the higher volume makes up for it.

We know that % of Sale can result in high dollar payouts due to the higher purchase price. There will be far fewer conversions, but the payout on those few can be a lot of money. There are offers out there that result in $3000 purchases. So, a 25% payout would be a check you'd love to see.

With this new knowledge, you should be getting excited about the opportunities in affiliate marketing. And, it's just the tip of the iceberg as far as the information and tools I'll be bringing to you in the rest of the book. I'm going to show you how to take all of the affiliate links, thousands of them that the advertisers supply through the networks, and put them out there on the Internet in the right places. You'll learn about Web sites, blogs and social networks for marketing.

I won't just throw you out there with a Web site and some blogs. I'll give you extensive knowledge in how to use PPC, marketing and CPM, as well as impressions marketing. These are the tools that will bring highly targeted visitors to your sites and blogs. They will arrive there with a need for more information or to order the product or service you're marketing. A simple click later money is in your bank account.

SECTION III
INTERNET ADVERTISING TO BRING SITE VISITORS

CHAPTER 1
PPC ("Pay per Click") Advertising

PPC advertising, also called CPC,("Cost Per Click"), advertising, is an extremely effective ad tool for the affiliate marketing business. Never before in advertising history could you:

- target a prospect so effectively
- tailor what the prospect sees to their precise interests
- take the prospect to the precise location of the offer tailored to their interests
- pay only when the prospect takes the action that you want
- measure results, right down to cost per conversion with a high degree of accuracy
- set an automated budget that isn't exceeded, even though your ads are running 24/7/365 without supervision

In PPC, you are bidding against competitor advertisers for clicks on the keywords or phrases you want. Later in this chapter, we'll go through the specifics of this bidding, and I'll show you how to get a better position for the same bid, or even a lower bid, than your competitors.

There are a few key components to marketing using PPC advertising, all of which are very important to the overall success of your campaign:

- targeted Keywords
- well-written targeted ads
- well-structured targeted landing pages

Without these three elements, plus a killer offer, all working together, your campaign will not be successful. One of the biggest reasons for failure is lack of knowledge. I am going to eliminate this factor by simply telling you what you need to know, right now.

Advertising in the Newspaper

A newspaper advertising sales person will give you demographics for their subscribers. They'll tell you how many newspapers they sell at vendor locations. They'll even give you subscriber income demographics in many cases. But when it all comes down to it, they can't give you documented proof that even 1% of those subscribers actually saw your ad last week. They can't tell you how many who did see it took action to give you business. Tracking this is left up to you.

It's not just how many saw your ad, but how many who really have any interest or need for your product or service. If you run an ad for a weight loss product or book, how many of the 100,000 readers of the paper are overweight? How many of that number care? How many of that number read the paper the day the ad ran? And, how many read the section in which you ran the ad? It's easy to see how you could take this scatter-gun approach, aim at your 100,000 prospects, and have only a hundred or so see your ad. And, out of that 100 or so, how many take action? Will you know how many later so you can decide if running another of these expensive ads is even worth it?

You have to ask every phone caller, and question every walk-in customer how they came to you. Few do this, and nobody can do it even close to 100% of the time. It's just too annoying to their customers. And who says they'll even remember accurately which ad or medium brought them? If you're running ads on TV, radio, newspapers and magazines, it's a nightmare to try and devise a system that even remotely comes close to determining which one brought in the customers for your last sale.

TV and Radio Advertising

Most newspapers do your ad layout for free as part of the ad run cost. Some radio and TV vendors will do the same in a very limited way. If you need on screen or voice talent, you'll pay extra for it, and that can be a lot of money. The time to take an idea from inception to the airwaves can be quite long. This forces you into running offers that you may have already decided aren't working because you are already under contract.

Back to our newspaper example. They don't call this mass advertising without good reason. You put your ad out on TV, and the station tells you that 100,000 people watch that show every Wednesday night. They don't tell you how many viewers mute the commercials. They don't tell you how many use the commercials as a break to make a sandwich. There is just no way to know how many people actually watched or listened to your commercial.

As far as measuring results with multiple campaigns are concerned, you face the same problem with newspapers. If you're running multiple campaigns in different media for one promotion (and that's the way we do it a lot of the time), then it becomes a logistical problem to try determining which worked the best at bringing in the customers. Basically, with newspapers you pay a lot of money, the ads run, and then you hope for results. If you get a pretty good turnout for your promotion, it's still unlikely that you'll be able to pin down which advertiser brought in the most revenue. Sure, coupons take care of this aspect, but they can't if you're running the same discounts in non-print media at the same time. So, you have to limit exposure and results just to measure results.

Magazines and Specialty Publishing

Magazines, local business maps, and combined full color glossy mall promotion pieces, all have a time lag between the moment that you make your purchase and the moment the piece hits the street. Magazines typically require advertisers to provide final ad layouts at least two months prior to print production. Maps can require an even longer period of time to prepare for print. Sometimes they're still out selling new ads a month after you've committed to your space.

There simply is no way to be proactive and respond to market and area events with these lead times. It isn't uncommon for a retailer to promote merchandise they perceive as slow moving, only to have the magazine ad come out when half the stock has been depleted due to heavier-than-expected seasonal volume. Talk about a waste of money! Though the customer coming in for that great spring dress deal may locate something else they will purchase, it doesn't make them happy with your advertising when the item that got the customer there in the first place is out of stock in their size.

PPC Advertising is Very Different from Traditional Methods

It's not that the traditional media and methods don't work, because they always do, but PPC advertising does everything that traditional methods do, but better, faster, cheaper, and with more measurable results.

Targeting Your Best Prospect

While others are using the scatter-gun approach, randomly shooting arrows into the air and hoping some of them hit the target, the PPC advertiser is defining their target customer, taking aim, and scoring a hit every time.

There is no guesswork to this process. At the end of this chapter, I'll give you access to the resources we will talk about here, but for now we want to learn why and how PPC marketing works so well and so economically. The first targeting strategy is to understand your prospect, their needs, desires, buying habits, etc. If you know the problem your product or service solves for them, or the enjoyment it brings, then the first step in your research is going to be much more productive.

Setting a Budget with Automatic Controls

Not only can you precisely target your prospect with PPC, you can control your advertising budget as well. It's not just setting a monthly budget for PPC. You can divide your budget by campaigns, ad groups, and even individual key phrases. You'll see later how this can increase your profits by allowing you to move your budget around, putting your dollars to work where they'll bring the greatest return.

You can instruct the search engine to limit your spending by the month, by the day, or even structure your ads to run only during certain times of day. If you tell *Google* to only allow you to place ads that cost you $200 per day, and you don't allocate that by ad, campaign or ad group, once you hit your budget, your ads will simply stop appearing in searches. New advertisers find this really helpful, as they are testing a lot of new ad variations, landing pages, and conversion rates. It's a lifesaver to be able to limit expense while testing, as you don't want to go broke figuring out that one campaign simply isn't converting for you.

Combining these precise spending controls with the ability to highly target your customer, there has never been a more effective marketing tool than PPC. What I'll teach you about PPC is not known or utilized by the majority of advertisers. This creates an opportunity for you to maximize profits while minimizing expense.

Keyword and Key Phrase Research

What is a keyword? In Internet usage, it is a word that denotes the theme of Web content, and one that someone would be likely to type into a search engine to locate the information, product or service they want. In actuality, using just one word usually results in too broad a search, turning up a lot of unrelated search results. An example would be the word "paint." Typing just that word into a search engine could yield:

- House paint
- Wall paint
- Artist's paint
- Acrylic paint
- Paint ponies
- "Paint Your Wagon"

There are probably a great many more matches that would not be of any interest to the searcher who really wanted only to buy some spray paint for plastic furniture. Therein is the importance of key *phrases*. Typing in *"plastic furniture spray paint"* would drastically limit the results, but that's good because it's what the searcher wanted in the first place.

So, as we go forward, I'll use the term *"key phrase"* most of the time, as it is more appropriate, and is how we'll get this targeting strategy honed to a fine edge. Our job is to understand our customer, make some assumptions and guesses as to their wants, needs and problems, and how they might go about searching for solutions in the Web search engines. This is called *"keyword research."* I'll put links to those we discuss here, and other places where you can do keyword research, at the end of the chapter. Right now, let's talk about what it is and how to do it.

Keyword Research and Selection

Let's use an example that isn't real, but allows some flexibility in our word selections. You are selling a product, or you're an affiliate marketer trying to get paid by sending a customer, and that product is *"blue widgets."* Now, you have a pretty good idea of the ways in which someone would search for blue widgets on the Web, including:

- Blue widgets
- Buy blue widget
- Blue widget pricing
- Blue widget information
- Best blue widgets
- Used blue widgets
- New blue widgets
- Locate blue widgets
- Blue widgets overstock
- Order blue widgets online

You're getting the idea. So, I go to several keyword research tools online, one example being *Google*'s keyword research tool. They all work the same, but they pull their information from their own search engine, meaning *Yahoo*'s search tool will give you information about *Yahoo* searches rather than *Google* searches. Others, like *WordTracker.com* track several engines. Anyway, the principle and process is the same:

1. Take your list of key phrases and enter them into the keyword tool.
2. Check the number of searches for each to see how much they are used.
3. For PPC, determine how stiff the competition is between advertisers to get a click on that phrase.
4. Let the tool suggest other key phrases you may not have thought about, and that show a good click history.
5. Choose the ones that fit your needs, content, advertiser, product or service the best and take them to the ad step later.

What might the search engine keyword tool suggest for your research that we may have missed? Perhaps there are more people out there than you would think that are interested in how blue widgets are made. They may or may not be customers, but you can't know, so that key phrase is one you would want to target on your landing pages because the tool says there are a lot of people using that phrase.

Definition: Landing Page – The Web page where a link takes a visitor. This could be the link in a PPC search ad, or any link you place in text anywhere. The page where they land is the *"landing page."*

Landing Pages and Their Importance

Consider the consumer who sees an ad for a great discount on picture hangers at a *Super Walmart* or *Home Depot*. These big box stores are so large that they have entrances widely spaced around the building. And they have a great number of very long aisles with merchandise. Picture hangers aren't a large item, and they could be really difficult to locate in this huge store. Even if they are there for other items, how long do you think they'll spend searching for the item before giving up and going home?

The first important thing to do is to think of your landing page, the place where your link takes the visitor from the search page, not as a store, but as an aisle. An even better suggestion is to think of it as a specific shelf on that aisle. You want the visitor to be directed to PRECISELY the spot where their picture hangars are sitting. Actually, the store has an advantage over your site. They may have driven several miles and are reluctant to leave without the item they came for. Not so with a Web site. They aren't going to have to get in their car and travel to another store. All they have to do is hit that BACK button to get back to the search list and try somewhere else.

Some would say you should build your ads first for PPC, and others would say the landing pages come first. I don't see how you can build an ad to send someone somewhere that doesn't exist, so get your site laid out, decide on what you're promoting, and design pages to pre-sell the visitor or get the click to the advertiser for your affiliate payment. Once the landing page is done, you can then target and word ads for it.

Let's tie a couple of things together here, landing pages and key phrases, and use our blue widgets example. Perhaps you have an advertiser offering a good payout if you get them a visitor who signs up for a free sample blue widget, or maybe it's a demo widget. You also see that the keyword research tool suggests that that there are people searching regularly for "how blue widgets are made." You didn't expect that one, but it's worth using in your marketing due to the search volume.

The fact that they want to know how they're made doesn't mean they want to buy one or more blue widgets now, but it certainly could mean that. So, you want to create a landing page that will convert for you and your adver- tiser based on the key phrase *"how blue widgets are made."* First, make that the title, or maybe *"How We Make Blue Widgets."* Let that visitor know right away that they've come to the right place, the right aisle in the store, and they're going to get what they want.

Now, we still want to believe that this interest in how they're made is related to a desire to buy blue widgets, so we don't want to leave out the pre-sell and affiliate link that gets us paid. After all, if you are about to buy some blue widgets, but you're concerned about quality of construction, you do this search. You are taken to this great page, maybe only having three or four hundred words, but it clearly explains how this company makes their widgets, and why it's a better process than that used by other companies. If you're convinced, and it's time to go ahead and buy, why wouldn't you use the link here to a free sample or a demo?

I'm going to tie the landing page concept into affiliate marketing success platforms later. I'll show you how each blog post is a landing page, how your Web site should be constructed to maximize traffic with focused landing pages, and more. Just remember a critical fact: it doesn't matter how much you spend to get a PPC click from a search engine, or how much you spend in any type of Web advertising to get someone to one of your sites, if they don't stay there and do what you need them to do to gener- ate a payout click to your advertiser, you've wasted your ad money.

The PPC Ad

The PPC ad is what the searchers see when they enter their search, and your ad is bid to show up for the key phrases they enter. These ads show up at the top and along the right margin on *Google*, and most other major search engine results pages.

Definition of SERP

When you're reading about search engines and getting better results, they're likely to use this acronym, which stands for "*Search Engine Results Pages.*" This is simply the page you see when you've entered your key phrase and hit the search button.

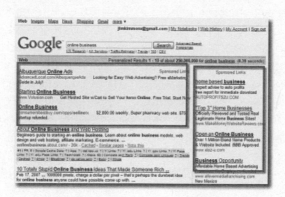

The image shows a *Google* SERP, and the PPC ads are in the bold border boxes. Though there are three at the top, this varies. Sometimes you'll see two, one, or even none at the top. Other search engines may use the right side, the top, or both to display paid ads. The results below the box on the left are the free results. Those are not paid for in any way. When we talk about SEO, you'll learn ways to move your results toward the top of the free results over time.

How does *Google* determine the order of its paid ads? First, we've already talked about bidding for key phrase placement, so that is obviously an important factor. However, it isn't all about the bid. Let's look at a screen shot of the *Google* keyword tool's estimation of bids for a set of key phrases for "*business cards.*"

Keywords	Estimated Avg. CPC ⑦	Advertiser Competition ⑦	Local Search Volume: May ⑦	Global Monthly Search Volume ⑦
Keywords related to term(s) entered - sorted by relevance ⑦				
business cards	$10.56		1,830,000	1,600,000
order business cards	$11.61		9,900	6,600
personal business cards	$7.65		Not enough data	9,900
discount business cards	$14.61		4,400	2,400
business cards design	$6.05		40,500	33,100
business cards designs	$4.70		5,400	5,400
print business cards	$7.72		49,500	33,100
business card	$6.04		2,240,000	1,830,000
business cards template	$3.69		9,900	9,900
business cards templates	$3.62		27,100	22,200

When you use *Google*'s keyword tool, it is designed to tell you how many searches are being done on the key phrase, as well as give you an idea of competition for that phrase among advertisers. There is also an estimated average CPC column. The green bars are all full in this shot, indicating high competition for these phrases. You can see that some of them have really large search volumes.

If we take discount business cards as an example, we also see that *Google* estimates the average cost being paid for each click to be $14.61. That's a lot of money, but it isn't what the smart advertisers are paying. You probably also noticed that the average CPC isn't related to the number of searches, which doesn't seem logical. You would think that more searches would correspond to higher cost if you get a click. But, it's all about the advertisers, as *Google*, as the other engines, doesn't set prices. They merely take the advertiser bids, add in some other criteria, and the ads appear, with billing going out to the advertisers.

So, just how do we know what we're going to be paying for any given key phrase or where we'll show up in the row of results? *Google* uses a quality score to determine where your ad is placed in the paid results. Here's what *Google*'s help page says about it:

How we determine Quality Scores for the content network:

A Quality Score is calculated for your ad each time it's eligible to appear on a content network placement. The following factors are considered:

- The relevance of the ad and keywords to the placement
- Your ad's performance history on that and similar placements
- The quality of your ad's landing page

What they're giving us is guidance on how to increase our affiliate marketing profits by getting better ad placement. But, there's also the cost factor. When your ad's quality score is better than that of a competitor, you can actually get a higher placement in the search results at a lower CPC than the competitor is paying. Why would *Google* give you more for less in their pocket?

It's because they're not really making less just because you're paying less. First, your CTR is taken into account. CTR (*"**C**lick-**T**hrough-**R**atio"*) is a simple mathematical relationship of the number of clicks your ad generates compared to the number of impressions, or times your ad is presented.

Example: In a certain week, your ad is presented 1000 times in searches, or gets 1000 impressions. Searchers actually click on it 65 times. Your CTR is 65/1000 = .065, or 6.5%.

Look at this from *Google*'s point of view. If your ad is able to get 6.5% of the people who see it to click on it, yet it's right now two positions below a competitor's ad with only a 4.5% CTR, then an adjustment is in order. CTR is a part of your ad's quality score for this reason. They aren't actually making less money overall if they move your ad up a notch above that competitor's ad at 4.5%. They are getting more clicks from your ad at a lower position, so there should be even more at a higher position. You can see how those *"not in the know,"* and writing poor ads that don't generate good CTR, can be pushed into much higher bids to get the position they want. Those much higher bids are part of that estimate of average CPC.

There's also the competition among search engines, and it's quite fierce. Searchers want to find what they want, when they want it, and don't want to waste time going to pages that don't meet their needs. When they find a search engine that delivers, they tend to stick with it. That's why the quality score looks at the relevance of your landing page as part of this secret score calculation. So, while your landing page is important in getting the site visitor to click on your offer link for payout, it's also important to make sure that it's highly relevant to your PPC ad wording so you can spend less for better position in the SERPs for paid ads.

In our example above, I can guarantee you that the smart advertisers are not paying $14 per click for great placement for *"discount business cards."* The smart advertisers have a highly relevant landing page. They have also created killer ad copy that makes their ad stand out and get more clicks, and their CTR is better than that of their competitors. That's what will move their ad up in the results.

One of the great things about PPC marketing is that it allows you to show your ads to only those people who are interested in them and then to only pay when those people click on your ad. Using this method simply means you only pay money for the customers you are sent. This certainly is a better option than just paying to be seen like every other advertising method I have mentioned. Remember, however, the importance of selecting the right keywords, and making sure the right audience sees your ad. Let's use another example.

Let's say I want to promote an offer for free business cards online. So I put together a Web site and I am ready to advertise. I head on over to *Google*. com, *Yahoo.com*, and MSN.com and set up PPC advertising accounts so I can begin reaching the people that use those search engines every day.

The search engine will ask me to enter the keyword phrases that will make my ad show up. What this means is any keyword I put in this box shown below will trigger my ad to appear if someone searches for that keyword on the search engine. Let's say we use these keywords: "*cards, free cards, cards online.*"

When someone types in the words above, they will see our ad. These words, however, are not very targeted. People looking for free business cards probably aren't going to type in "*cards*" or "*cards online.*" People typing in these keywords could be looking for free greeting cards, free poker cards, or anything of that nature. A better list of keywords for this ad would be:

Keywords: free business cards, business cards, cheap business cards

Here we know the people typing in these keywords are interested in what we have, so we know we have a great chance to gain a customer. This is just targeting your audience very specifically, and that's exactly what PPC advertising offers you that many other forms of advertising simply can't offer.

Targeting your audience like this with very specific keywords accomplishes two things:

1. Reduces advertising cost
2. Increases click through ratios

Your advertising costs decrease simply because you aren't showing your ad to people that click on it and then leave because they were never interested in what you had to offer in the first place. Making sure you target your audience as specifically as you possibly can is one of the major keys to success in affiliate marketing, and in using the PPC method to gain customers.

Your click through ratio on your ads will certainly increase, which means you get more customers, and at a lower cost. If you're showing ads to people that have no interest in what the ad is describing it's likely they won't click on it. However, if you are showing someone interested in free business cards an ad about free business cards you have a much greater chance of getting the customer to take action, click on your ad, and come to your Web site. Most PPC search engines will actually decrease your cost per click if you have an increased CTR so it actually pays to write relevant ads and show them to relevant people.

What Makes a Killer Ad – Getting Better CTR

The wording of our PPC ad is critical to our income, we want to make sure that we understand the searcher's motivation and how to get them to click.Wording influences our profits in more than one respect. Doing a good job with the ad words and phrasing increases our CTR, thus we get a higher quality score, more clicks at a lower cost each, and more people to our site to take the action we need for our payout. Look back at the SERP, and you'll see that there are a lot of ads along that right side, and two or three usually at the top.

We have a couple of seconds to get that searcher's attention to our ad. Our headline and brief text is all we have to influence them. Since we can't see what any specific competitor is bidding and paying for their placement in the paid results, it's sometimes hard to determine why one ad is positioned higher than another, even if their wording is poor.

There is another cost strategy in play here as well. A PPC consultant who has done comparison costing for his own accounts found that for many key phrase searches, the cost difference between position 3 or 4 and position 1 or 2 can be really large.

Here's a screen shot from _Google_'s report to an advertiser about CPC and average position of the ads:

	Summary		Keywords		Placements ⑦	A

	Clicks	Impr.	CTR	Avg. CPC	Cost	Avg. Pos	Conv. Rate	Cost/Conv.
	3,650	66,922	5.45%	$0.95	$3,468.51	2.5	0.41%	$230.08
	3,286	49,837	6.59%	$0.98	$3,205.95	2.8	0.46%	$212.57
	364	17,085	2.13%	$0.72	$262.56	1.7	0.00%	$0.00
	0	984	0.00%	$0.00	$0.00	n/a	0.00%	$0.00
	0	984	0.00%	$0.00	$0.00	n/a	0.00%	$0.00

The key phrases don't matter for this example. What we want to see is the average position of the ads. This means that, over time, the top two ads ran between the 2nd and 3rd positions, with 2.5 – 2.8 in this column. Notice also that the CTRs for these ads were pretty good, at more than 5%. Remember that this means that 5 or more out of every 100 people who saw these ads clicked on them.

This person shared with us that he watched these reports with the specific goal of keeping his ads somewhere around position 3 or 4. If there were two or three ads at the top, this kept his ads at the top of the right side, now and then getting the bottom position in the top ads. What his studies showed, with a few discreet inquiries among his friendly competitors, was that he was paying $2 less per click than the competitors in the top two positions consistently. The importance of this is to understand that his CTR would have been much higher than those above him to hold his position over time at a much lower cost per click. In fact, his cost averaged $1.75 per click, less than half of what the top two were paying.

So, what makes a killer ad, generating higher CTR, lower cost, and more clicks? Well, as affiliate marketers, we throw in one more criteria as well; encourages the click, but also increases the click on our landing page that brings us a payout. In other words, just getting visitors to our landing page at a lower cost and in greater numbers is fine, but if they don't take the next step, we get no income. So, when we word our ads, we should consider this. Don't think that just wording an ad that gets a high CTR will necessarily get us any payouts. It will make the search engine happy, as it is paid for the click to our site, but we're not making money.

Here's what *Google* says about good ads:

After all, *Google*, *Yahoo*, MSN, *Bing*, and all of the other search engines

As a basic rule, use clear, well-written, and specific ad text that highlights the differentiating characteristics of your product or service. Below are some more specific tips to help you create compelling ad text.

Create simple, enticing ads.
What makes your product or service stand out from your competitors? Highlight these key differentiating points in your ad. Be sure to describe any unique features or promotions you offer.

Include prices and promotions.
The more information about your product that a user can gain from your ad text, the better. For example, if a user sees the price of a product and still clicks the ad, you know they're interested in a potential purchase at that price. If they don't like the price, they won't click your ad, and you save yourself the cost of that click.

Use a strong call-to-action.
Your ad should convey a call-to-action along with the benefits of your product or service. A call-to-action encourages users to click on your ad and ensures they understand exactly what you expect them to do when they reach your landing page. Some call-to-action phrases are *Buy, Purchase, Call today, Order, Browse, Sign up,* and *Get a quote;* while 'find' and 'search' may be accurate verbs, they imply that the user is still in the research mode, and may not encourage the user to perform the action you'd most like them to take.

Include one of your keywords in your ad text.
Find the best performing keyword in your ad group and include it in your ad text, especially in the title. Whenever a user types that keyword and sees your ad, the keyword phrase will appear in <u>bold font</u> within your ad on Google. This helps draw the user's attention to your ad and shows users that your ad relates to their search.

Choose the best destination URL.
Review the website you're advertising and find the specific page that has the information or product described in your ad. If users do not find what is promised as soon as they arrive, they are more likely to leave your website. Be sure that any promotions and particular products mentioned in your ad are visible on your landing page.

Test multiple ads in each ad group.
Experiment with different offers and call-to-action phrases to see what's most effective for your advertising goals. Our system automatically <u>rotates ads</u> within an ad group and shows the better-performing ad more often.

want you to be successful at PPC. It's their income stream, and a really big one. *Yahoo* uses a quality scoring system similar to *Google* to rank PPC ads. The point is that the chain of PPC profits for your affiliate marketing PPC accounts must have all of the links in place:

- a strong knowledge of your target prospect.
- careful research and keyword/key phrase selection.
- a highly relevant landing page .
- an ad worded properly for relevance & eye-catching for getting that click.
- research and constant PPC account reports monitoring for ad position and performance relative to cost.

All of the actions I'm giving you tie together for success. Our PPC consultant also carefully kept track of performance related to ad position. He found that it didn't take the search engine long to assess the performance of his ads and begin to reward his efforts. You can't look for overnight results, but his tracking showed that better positioning and lower cost began to show up within a few weeks. His best key phrases started out with CPC of $2.93. Within a month or so, the very same ad, showing a CTR of more than 6%, was rewarded by *Google* with a move up from position around 6 or 7 to a 5 position, and drop in CPC to around $2.25.

A few more weeks passed, with a continued good CTR, and the ad moved up to position 4. The cost however, went down to under $2 per click, settling in at around $1.75 per click, and hanging in at the 2.8 average position in the screen shot. Because you'll likely be doing a lot of PPC, you can see how just the wording of your ads can cut your marketing costs by a huge amount. But it doesn't stop there.

Check the *Google* help text box above again. They suggest call-to-action words in the ad, like "*buy, purchase, call today, order, browse, sign up*", etc. If the searcher actually clicks on your ad with words like these in it, it's far more likely that they'll be taking the next action you need to get your income. The search engine gets theirs with the first click, but you need the second one to get your payout.

We don't know how much research the prospect has been doing before this search. They may have done a lot. Now, they see your ad, and it has "*order free business cards*" in your ad title and/or text. They are ready to do just that. Your advertiser is paying you CPA for the form they'll fill out to get that teaser order of free business cards. If they click from the search page, they're doing it because your ad tells them they can order, so it's highly likely that they will. Of course, remember our previous discussion about the types of forms and how requiring too much information can cut your conversions dramatically. In this instance however, the prospect will expect to have to enter their address and other information, otherwise they can't get their free business cards shipped.

Keyword Selection & Ad Wording Example

I've given you a lot of information and examples in the previous pages, but let's make sure you have a firm understanding with some screen shots of the *Google* Keyword Tool and how we would select key phrases for a landing page and how we might word our ads. I went to the *Google* Keyword Tool and entered *"free business cards."*

Then, I changed one thing. Notice the word *"Broad"* in the box at the

Keywords	Estimated Avg. CPC	Advertiser Competition	Local Search Volume: May	Global Monthly Search Volume	Match type: Broad
Keywords related to term(s) entered - sorted by relevance					
free business cards templates	$4.14		12,100	5,400	Add
create free business cards	$4.62		6,600	3,600	Add
free business cards design	$3.81		5,400	2,900	Add
business card free	$3.64		165,000	110,000	Add
free business cards	$7.40		201,000	165,000	Add
business cards for free	$4.65		18,100	8,100	Add
free business cards printing	$5.36		2,400	880	Add
print free business cards	$4.87		12,100	6,600	Add
free business cards program	$3.46		880	590	Add
free business cards template	$3.38		1,900	1,900	Add
free online business cards	$5.02		12,100	6,600	Add
make business cards free	$4.47		12,100	5,400	Add
free printable business cards	$3.43		12,100	8,100	Add

upper right of the results. Let's talk about what you can specify to the search engine as to how the keywords are entered, and whether you want your ad to display or not.

Broad Match

This means that the words you specify can be entered in any order, with any words in between, and your ad will still be presented. In other words, the *"free business cards"* I asked for could be entered *as "business free cards," "business cards free",* or even *"is there a free place I can get cards for my business?"* For many of your ads, this broad match may be OK, but you may want to consider, based on the offer and other factors, one of the other match types.

Phrase Match

By putting the phrase into quotation marks, as *"free business cards,"* you tell the engine that you want the words in the phrase searched in the order you show them. However, there can still be other words around the phrase. So, *"is there a free place for business cards,"* though the words are in the right order, wouldn't display your ad because there are words in between. But, *"<u>find</u> free business card offers"* would display your ad.

Exact Match

We're getting more restrictive as we tell the engine that we only want our ad to display if the searcher types in *"free business cards"* exactly that way, in that word order, and with no other words in the search. This is generally not a selection you'll make, as you can see from some of the examples, you would likely lose some good prospects this way.

Most of your phrases will be best covered with either *"broad"* or *"phrase"* match. You can run tests of your conversion rates with both. That's both your conversion from the search engine, and your conversion to a payout at your landing page.

Here's what the above keyword screen displays with *"phrase"* selected:

Keywords	Estimated Avg. CPC	Advertiser Competition	Local Search Volume: May	Global Monthly Search Volume	Match Type: Phrase
Keywords related to term(s) entered - sorted by relevance					
"free business cards templates"	$4.14		2,400	2,400	Add Phrase
"create free business cards"	$4.52		1,600	1,200	Add Phrase
"free business cards design"	$3.81		880	480	Add Phrase
"business card free"	$3.64		27,100	8,100	Add Phrase
"free business cards"	$7.40		110,000	110,000	Add Phrase
"business cards for free"	$4.65		5,400	2,400	Add Phrase
"free business cards printing"	$5.36		880	170	Add Phrase
"print free business cards"	$4.87		4,400	2,900	Add Phrase
"free business cards program"	$3.46		320	140	Add Phrase
"free business cards template"	$3.38		590	590	Add Phrase
"free online business cards"	$6.02		2,400	1,300	Add Phrase
"make business cards free"	$4.47		1,600	1,000	Add Phrase
"free printable business cards"	$3.43		8,100	6,600	Add Phrase

Notice how the more restrictive requirement of the words being together and in that order cuts down on the number of searches. This isn't necessarily bad, as a big part of our job is trying to tightly target our results to the prospects most likely to take the action we require in order for us to get paid. Note that the difference in placing the quotation marks around *free business cards* cuts the number of searches almost in half.

Over time, you'll gain experience in relating broad and phrase match with both your key phrases and the product or offering to get the best results. More searches may equal more clicks to your landing page, but if these clicks don't result in a payout to you, the money you've spent is wasted. It's a balance between volume and quality of clicks from the search engine.

Our Free Business Cards Landing Page

Before we set up our ads, let's discuss our landing page briefly. There are a many offers, from a number of vendors that we might be looking at for our campaign. We could be using a Web page, a blog post, or a review site to get the visitor to take the action we need for our money. But for this example, we really need to know where we're sending the searcher when they click and what's there, so we can word our ads appropriately.

Let's say that we have multiple offers available to us from various business card vendors. These offers are comparable in value to us, with some being CPL, and others CPA. We decide that for this campaign, we're going to do a review site format, with comments on the offerings and cards of multiple vendors. This is fun, because we'll get paid no matter which vendor wins the click from our review page.

We do a short review of each vendor and their free card offer. Perhaps we compare things like the quantity you get free, with upgrades offered, upgrade costs, delivery time, and other things that would be of interest. At any rate, we end up with a bit of text about each vendor's free business card offer. Note that you'll want to use that *"free business cards"* phrase in each review for relevance. The search engine will give you credit for that in computing your ad's quality score. A link, button or image link to the vendor's page is with each review. No matter which they select, we get paid if they follow through.

Designing Your Ad –
Get the Wording Right by Testing

With most of the search engines, you can run multiple ads for each key phrase, allowing you to test the CTR of the ads against each other. Allowing several to run for a while, you can settle in on one or two that result in the very best CTR.

You can probably come up with more, but these are examples of how you can change the wording of an ad to change its focus. If someone is shopping, and they value getting it done quickly and easily, then the *"Free Business Cards Fast"* ad just might grab their attention and a click.

With *Google*, we only get 25 characters for the title and 35 characters for each of the two description lines. So, creativity and headline punch required to make your ad stand out from the others. The good news is that you don't pay unless you get a click, so setting up these ads for this offer and landing page would not cost you a dime extra. You just learn which do the job best for CTR, eliminating the rest.

You will be able to keep track of the CTR by the ad variation, which will help you see which ads get the greatest number of visitors click through to your landing page. But don't stop there. Carry your analysis over to conversions. You really need to develop more than one landing page, even if the variations between them aren't that great. By pointing different ads at different landing pages, you can determine which ads result in the money-click that gets you a payout.

An example might help. Using our free business cards, we may test the two ads comparing card offers for a review landing page. We should do two variations of that landing page, with one ad going to each. Otherwise, if the two ads are both doing a reasonable job of conversion to a click from the search, we will be unable to determine if one of them actually results in more clicks to your vendor and your payout.

What if they both get similar CTRs, but one is getting more secondary conversions, the one that results in money for us? Something in the ad wording may be preparing the prospect better for the offers, or for a decision to make a purchase or get the freebie. Testing the ads against each other for both phases of our process can make a difference in our profits. This secondary testing can be saved for later, and only used when two ads produce similar CTR from the search page.

Results Tracking for Decision-Making

Don't think it's a done deal when you've completed your testing, selected your best performing ads, and got visitors to your landing pages. The process never ends, because consumers are always changing their attitudes, preferences and buying habits. There are also outside influences at work. Vendors change their products and services. News and social influences can provide the opportunity to change ads or develop new ones to respond to current trends.

								1 - 6 of 6 keywords
Clicks	Impr.	CTR	Avg. CPC	Cost	Avg. Pos	Conv. Rate	Cost/Conv.	Conversions
1,681	34,815	4.83%	$0.84	$1,405.36	3.0	0.30%	$279.65	5
279	16,875	1.65%	$0.97	$269.87	1.4	0.72%	$134.94	2
1,030	8,788	11.72%	$1.17	$1,200.68	2.4	0.68%	$170.42	7
467	4,038	11.57%	$0.87	$407.88	3.0	0.22%	$407.26	1
193	2,406	8.02%	$0.96	$184.72	2.2	0.00%	$0.00	0

Above is a partial screen shot of a *Google* A*dwords* report page, with the results over a period of time for five key phrases. We just want to see how to use these numbers to make decisions so the specific product or phrases don't matter. It does help to know that this is a high ticket item, so you don't get the wrong idea about the small number of conversions in relation to the money being spent on clicks. This marketer was making good money on this campaign, as the product paid on a % of Sale basis, and the payout was between $1,000 and $2,000 for each conversion.

Let's concentrate on the first and third lines, with the 1,681 and 1,030 click numbers. The two key phrases for these items were obviously focused on the offer and product, but differ in several respects. Notice that the average position on the SERPs wasn't that different, at 3.0 and 2.4 respectively. But, one of them has a CTR of 11.72%, while the other is only 4.83%.

If we were only looking at the Average CPC, then the phrase costing us $1.17 might look less appetizing than the one that cost $0.84. And we got a lot more clicks at the lower CPC as well. In fact, we only spent 17% more total dollars ($205 more) to get 53% (651) more clicks at the lower price. If that were the whole story, then our decision could very well be to concentrate our dollars on the top item, getting more clicks for less CPC. But there's more. Now look at the columns for *"conversion rate"* and *"cost per conversion."* Though we're paying more for every click, we are getting more than double the conversion rate, and our cost per conversion is $109 less. That's because we converted 7 of the higher priced key phrase clicks versus 5 at the lower cost. This changes our thought process significantly. Actually, we want to keep both of these key phrases going, and may want to kill a couple of the low performers, or at least lower their budget, moving more budget to the two top performers.

We might want to temporarily pause the bottom two phrases, moving that $500+ of budget to higher bids or more click purchases for the top performers. This one action might increase our income by thousands of dollars, while spending the same amount on clicks as before. The point is that we never want to ignore our campaign reports, and we always want to be watching performance by campaign and by key phrase. Decisions like the ones in this example make a huge difference in our income.

Bringing It All Together for PPC

Let's recap what we've learned about PPC marketing. It's critical to your future success in affiliate marketing that you thoroughly understand it, and how to use PPC to your advantage without breaking the bank. When you hear others knocking PPC as a waste of money, It's because they never learned the principles I've given you here. They expect a lot for a little, don't do their research, and they don't test and follow up with results tracking.

Targeted Prospects with Precise Budget Control

Newspapers, magazines, TV and radio provide audience and reader demographics, but they can't tell who actually saw your high dollar ad. And it's very difficult to track the leads from these sources to an income event. You spend a lot of money for results that you can't track and can't evaluate accurately over time.

PPC gives you the ability to accurately target a very narrow segment of the populace based on the likelihood that they want what you're offering. You can get your ad in front of this targeted group in a budget that you set, and it's automatically enforced. And, the greatest thing of all...you don't pay unless they click and arrive at your offer landing page.

Keyword and Key Phrase Selection

We've learned how to research keywords and key phrases that our target consumers use to locate information, or purchase, the products and services in our offers. I've shown you how to evaluate these key phrases so that you can concentrate on those promising the greatest return on your marketing investment.

Quality Landing Pages are Critical

No matter how well you select key phrases, and how many clicks you get from the search engine to your landing page, if visitors don't take the next action, your click payment was wasted. They must go on to take the action that results in your payout from the vendor.

Creating a landing page that gets the next click for income is just part of the job. Remember that your ad's quality score is partially based on the relevance of your landing page to the wording of your ad. A higher quality score gets your ad moved up higher in the results. But even better, you move higher, but at a lower CPC and you can get a higher position than a competing ad, and pay less for each click, because your CTR is better.

Ad Wording & Ad Variation Testing is Important

The competition for the searcher's click from the SERP is intense. Your window of opportunity to get a searcher to notice and click on your ad while its amongst the dozens on the page. It's the wording and phrasing of your ad that makes the difference. Though you don't pay unless they click, a huge amount of effort required to get a large number of impressions. If searchers don't click through to your landing page, you've wasted your time.

The better you do with ad wording, the better your CTR. And your quality score goes up with this CTR performance. So, as we discussed, landing pages with better quality score results are in better positions at lower costs per click.

Continually Track Results and Adapt

The fact that a key phrase works well this month doesn't mean it will next month. After a period of time, there is detailed reporting data allows you to compare campaigns, ad groups and individual key phrases for their relative performance. Nobody gets it right the first time, and nobody knows what's right until the data comes in.

Carefully analyze your report data. Compare not only CTR for key phrases, but CPC and conversion rates as well. We've seen that a higher CPC can be very profitable, because the conversion rates from that key phrase are much higher than for a lower cost phrase click. Track your results, making decisions based on hard data, not guesses.

RESOURCE LINKS

Here are links to search engine PPC sites, keyword research tools, and other Internet resources to help you get your PPC up and running.

Google Adwords:
http://google.com/adwords

Yahoo Search Marketing:
http://searchmarketing.yahoo.com

Microsoft AdCenter:
http://adcenter.microsoft.com

WordTracker Keyword Research:
http://wordtracker.com

Google Keyword Research Tool:
https://adwords.google.com/select/KeywordToolExternal

Success Story # 4 – Adrian Morrison

When I was in college, I spent a great deal of my free time playing Xbox 360 and socializing with friends. At the same time, I'm watching Anthony generate a lot of money online. Everyone who knew him could see that he was very successful at what he was doing, and that he was creating wealth others his age could only watch and dream about.

One day, between games, I decided that I wanted more out of life, and asked Anthony if I could do what he was doing in business. He was quite sure that it was within my reach, and jumped right into teaching me the tools and systems he was using. Once I put away the games, I was motivated and took in everything as quickly as he could share it with me.

I didn't jump right into huge amounts of income, with the business getting off to a slow but steady start. I was generating a few hundred dollars a month, but that was great for a college kid whose alternative was waiting tables. This few hundred dollars each month was a motivator, and I really got serious about applying myself and Anthony's process for even better results.

As this book is written, I'm 24 years old, and I've been applying Anthony's systems to my business for about a year and a half. My last month's check was $75,000! I can't tell you how excited I am, or how thankful that I listened to what Anthony had to say. All I had to do was apply it, as he gave me all of the tools and information I needed to be successful.

This isn't a "get rich quick" process, as it took me a year and a half to get to that $75,000 check, but it sure beats the heck out of a 9 to 5 job, and nobody's hiring out there anyway. It's work, but its fun, too. The money I've made has allowed me to not only put $150,000 into savings, but also to buy a Jaguar and an Escalade.

What Anthony taught me, and the success it has brought, has given me the knowledge and confidence to start a new online business recently. It's all about knowledge, confidence and motivation. I think that anyone reading this book should pay close attention to what he says and follow his techniques. They worked for me, and they can work for anyone else.

CPM Marketing

CPM stands for *("Cost Per Thousand")* It's not a typo, as the M in CPM is the Roman numeral for 1,000. The major difference in PPC and CPM is that CPM advertisers pay for their ad to be seen, whether it is clicked on or not. Since we really liked the fact that PPC allows us to only spend money if we actually get a visitor to our site, why would we want to do CPM, paying whether they click on the ad or not?

The main reason is that a vast number of great Web sites do not allow PPC marketing, only taking CPM ads for display. Do we care, or need, to market our offers on these Web sites? Sure we do. It's because the sites we select will have high traffic numbers, and we'll select them because this traffic is from a demographic or market segment that consists of prospects we want.

Some Definitions You'll Need to Know

CPM Advertising – Paying a Web site a certain amount for every 1,000 impressions or presentations of their ad. This is whether or not the visitor pays attention to the ad or takes action by clicking it. Each time the page loads for a site visitor, it counts as an impression. You determine how much you're willing to pay per thousand impressions, but the site also has a rate it wants to charge. You will negotiate the rate down to what you want to pay.

Creative - This is the visual ad that you or those you hire create for display. It is mostly image, with some text, and even motion in more cases now than in the past.

Frequency Cap - Many people visit a site more than once every day. Also, your ads may show on various pages when they load. For this reason, some people can be exposed to your ad multiple times in one day.

A frequency cap is set when you tell the site that you only want a visitor to see your ad a certain number of times, then it shouldn't display again for that visitor in a 24 hour period.

We can get a better idea of CPM advertising by a comparison with traditional media. Let's look at two popular types of traditional marketing that are heavily used, and how they compare to CPM on the Internet.

Magazines

Most magazines are published around themes or very specific topical material.

- An area, city or state
- Health and beauty
- Hobbies and crafts
- Age groups, retirees, etc.
- Lifestyle and entertainment

If you have a narrow focus on a topic or human endeavor, you will have a readership that is focused and will share common interests. When those interests align with an advertiser's products or services, you have a match for marketing. In our list above, a dramatic example would be a magazine targeted at retirees, or that age group. Ads with medical products that address aging issues, as well as ads with vacation offers and retirement homes in resort areas, though they are very different products, are very well-suited for each other and to the focus of this particular magazine.

Billboards

Driving down a major highway on our way into Las Vegas, Nevada, what kind of billboard advertising do you think we'll see the most? It will be the casinos, no doubt about it. This is location-based marketing, with the knowledge that a great number of automobiles will pass these billboards every day. And a great many of these cars will be headed to Las Vegas for entertainment and gambling.

The cost of this type of advertising is high, considering you're paying whether or not the billboard is read. But, the results definitely justify the expense. The casinos know that, even if they weren't on the visitor's agenda before they started their trip, the right message on a billboard assures them a visit from a vacationer while they're there.

CPM on the Web is the Same Concept

Magazine and billboard advertising is still around because it works. This type of reader targeting works on the Internet as well. Think of Web sites as either a magazine or a destination. People are both arriving at a site, and they're reading what they find there.

Magazine-like Sites

There are literally millions of these" *would-be"* sites, with themes or topics that run throughout their content Using our retirees again as an example, *AARP.org* draws a huge amount of traffic with common interests. Here are a few examples of CPM creatives running on one page of this site:

These advertisers are paying just to have their ads seen on this site, because they know that this site's readership travels a lot, thus uses rental cars. They also know that discount insurance targeted to this age group is a great draw for customers.

When looking at these ad creatives, it's a good time to make sure that you understand the importance of the creative, and your choices regarding images that you use. Unlike text ads and PPC, a large part of any success you enjoy with CPM advertising will come about from your creatives, as much as from how much you pay per thousand for impressions. After all, your ad is going to appear on a site with its own design, background colors, and density of content. It is critical that your ad stands out, or **"POPS"** to get the attention of the site visitor.

Unlike PPC, in which a person viewing the search page entered a specific keyword phrase indicating they want to find information on it or to locate and buy a product or service, your CPM ad is displayed without being requested by a searcher. They are on the site for their own reasons, and your ad must be not only related to the content of the site, it must catch their attention and stimulate their interest.

How to Find the Right Place to Advertise

Success with CPM advertising relies on some of the same things as PPC. We must get one click that brings a visitor to our offer or landing page, and then we need to get another one on an offer so that we get paid. The second click situation is pretty much the same in PPC and CPM, as our landing page must be highly relevant to our ad, and it must do a good job of getting the payout click.

The difference in PPC and CPM is at the front end. With CPM, we're working for a click from someone who isn't necessarily even thinking about our product or offering. They are on a site that draws our ideal customer, but they aren't necessarily shopping at all. For this reason, we must choose sites that are the very best, and the best means those with high traffic from our targeted consumer.

An example would be our offer of a weight loss product. There's no doubt that weight loss is a topic of interest mostly with women. So, placing our ad on a mechanic tool site would be a monumental waste of money. I'm not picking on anyone, as an offer of a discount on a chain saw would not do much good on a romance novel review site.

Sites with Similar Offer Ads

First, go around the Web, and locate sites that have ads for products and services that we are offering. Find other weight loss ads, and jot down or copy out the URL for that site as a possible venue for our weight loss ads. Get as many as you can, then get this next list.

Sites You Think Would be Visited by Your Target Audience

Don't assume that sites without weight loss ads aren't of value to your offer. That's assuming that everyone out there is super-educated in CPM marketing, and they're not. You will be, and you'll likely locate some excellent sites for your offers. Sometimes doing this will also get you some really great CPM rates, as the site isn't being inundated with marketers for your products.

A Tool to Get it Done Faster and Well is *Quantcast*

Quantcast.com is a site dedicated to Internet demographics, which is precisely what you need. I did some quick entry of my idea of who would make a good prospect for weight loss offers:

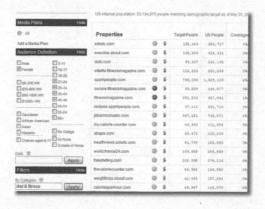

This is a partial screen shot showing results provided when I entered criteria like female, age groups, and the category *"diet & fitness."* I don't know enough yet to really figure out age groups, but this makes it easy to keep trying different criteria and comparing the results. The green dollar sign indicates that the site in that row accepts advertising.

Look at that list of potential sites, and we've barely begun our research! Working our way through different criteria, and testing site results by education and other factors, we can come up with a list of potential sites for our CPM ads. Visit each site, and see if there are already weight loss ads, and how many of them there are. It's not yet time to contact their advertising people yet for costs. We'll get to that later.

Learn All About a Site with *Quantcast.com*

There is a huge amount of valuable information to help you select sites that will provide a targeted audience for your ads, as well as help you to find other sites with similar content or overlapping interests for more ad placements. Let's look at some screen shots from *Quantcast* that analyze *www.perezhilton.com*.

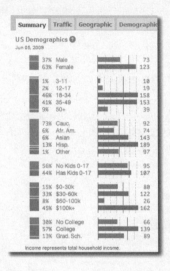

If we have an offer that we believe is suited to presentation on this site, what kind of information can we get to help us in our decision? Screen shots are portions of different screens.

In this first shot, we see a breakout of the more than 3.8 million U.S. site visitors by demographic information. Age, gender, income, and other factors will help us to determine if the visitors to this site are suited to our offer.

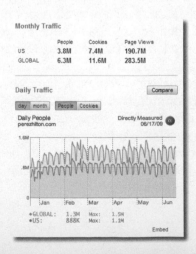

We also get monthly and daily site visitor statistics, page views, as well as the number of times a cookie was set in their computer. From *Wikipedia*: *"In computing, a **cookie** (also **browser cookie**, **computer cookie**, **tracking cookie**, **Web cookie**, **internet cookie**, and **HTTP cookie**) is a small string of text stored on a user's computer by a Web browser. A cookie consists of one or more name-value pairs containing bits of information such as user preferences, shopping cart contents, the identifier for a server-based session, or other data used by Web sites."*

Audience Also Likes ❓	
The people who visit perezhilton.com are also likely to visit these categories and sites:	
	Affinity
News/Information	
Star Magazine	54.1x
TMZ	48.8x
Pop Sugar	38.9x
The Superficial	38.5x
TV	
E! Online	28.5x
Bravo	19.1x
MTV	12.2x
tvsquad.com	11.1x
Regional/Local News	
lvrj.com	21.3x
New York Post	20.3x
NY Daily News	16.1x
Los Angeles Times	11.7x

Audience Also Visits ❓	
The people who visit perezhilton.com are also likely to visit:	
	Affinity
dlisted.com	73.2x
jossip.com	59.5x
towleroad.com	58.3x
gumgum.com	56.7x
showbizspy.com	54.1x
starmagazine.com	54.1x
x17online.com	53.6x
laineygossip.com	53.2x
lifeandstylemag.com	49.6x
tmz.com	48.8x
entertainmentandshow...	48.8x
ok-magazine.com	47.2x
goodplasticsurgery.c...	46.5x
wesmirch.com	46.5x
gossiprocks.com	45.4x

These two portions of the screen are really valuable tools for the affiliate marketer in locating sites for CPM ad placement. The left box shows similar categories frequented by these site visitors. But, even better, the right box shows us actual Web sites that the visitors to perezhilton.com also visited, and they are ranked by affinity, or how many crossed over to these sites.

You can see that we can find some great sites for our CPM that may be overlooked by some of our competitors. We can also make comparisons between these sites on *Quantcast* to more closely target our audience. It may be that one of these sites will better suit us once we examine the demographics. Suppose our product is related to women, and one of these related sites has a higher percentage of women than men as visitors than this one?

This site even shows you size and placement of the ads you're researching. *Quantcast* tells you who, how many, visitor characteristics, and even shows you where the ads are placed. This is all highly valuable information for the CPM affiliate marketer.

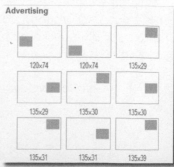

Advertising

Spending a lot of time on *Quantcast.com* is well worth it for the CPM affiliate marketer. This site will help you tightly target the sites that will bring you the highest impressions. Then you can create ads that will bring the CTR you need for conversions to payouts.

Killer "Creatives" Increase Your CTR

Unlike PPC, with CTR we're paying every time our ad is shown, whether the visitor clicks on it or not. Let's look at an example CPM and how we can blow the budget or make a profit based on the quality of our creatives.

$4.00 CPM is our cost – We have agreed to pay this site $4.00 for every 1000 times our ad is displayed, or for each impression. It's not a stretch to experience a CTR of only .01% in this type of marketing. Yes, that's only 1 click for every 1000 impressions, or 100 clicks for the $400 cost of 100,000 impressions. That's $4.00 per click, a pretty high rate.

I'm not saying that this is unacceptable for all offers, but it's going to take a big payout to make it worthwhile. After all, of this, 100 clicks do not guarantee any income once they get to your landing page and your offer. But, it's not a reason to drop this site if you can make an improvement on the front end. By increasing your CTR, you can cut into this cost, and maybe at some point, bring the CTR up to a point where the cost is not an obstacle.

This is where the quality of your creative can make a huge difference. What if you could increase the CTR for this site by 50%? It is quite possible, as the graphics, colors, text, and motion you usein a creative can have a huge impact on the CTR. This site might end up being an amazing revenue source if you could get the CPC down to $2.00 or less per click.

What are your considerations in developing a killer creative? Some of it is just common sense. Look where the ad will appear. Pay attention to the site layout, background color, text fonts and sizes, etc. After all, if the site has a baby-blue background, and you design a really great ad with the same color, it will disappear. Invisible ads don't generate clicks.

Grabbing attention with your ad is important, but clashing with the site theme and design isn't always the best approach either. It's a balance between fitting into the site's design while, grabbing attention with color, text, motion, or a combination.

Don't Put the Creative Cart before the Horse

Designing your creatives is quite important, but don't be in a hurry. I've just told you that you need to fit into the site's theme, but stand out for attention as well. You need to know where you're advertising before you can design the ads you'll be placing there. Do thorough research with *Quantcast* and other tools to determine where you're going to place your ads, then design the ads accordingly?

There aren't that many of us who are business-minded, good at marketing, Web design experts, and artistic as well. For this reason, you may be hiring an expert to design your ads. In the coming chapters, I'll give you details on how to use these professionals, but for now, know that freelance sites like *Elance.com* and *Guru.com* provide the talent you need at an affordable price. I'll show you how to use those sites to locate talent, get bids on your projects, and make sure that you get what you want before you pay.

Since many of you will be outsourcing some or all of your creative design, you can see that it's important to have your decisions made about site selection for advertising. Because you can't nail the most effective creative the first try, I recommend five or so for each ad. Test them to determine which one works best, or end up with a few that consistently provide the CTR you want. If you're going to pay to have five ads designed for an offer, having the site selected first guarantees that your ad design and colors are suitable. You don't want to pay to modify the ads because you designed first and selected sites second.

How to Test Before You Test!

Is that right? Yes, you can pre-test your ads before you test them on the actual site you've chosen for your CPM advertising. After all, to do CPM on a site with high traffic, you'll usually be negotiating CPM rates and frequency caps, then signing contracts. That's a lot of energy expended, not to mention any commitments made in the contracts. So, how can we get a firmer grip on what will be effective for ads and offers before we go this far?

In addition to PPC advertising, *Google* has a content network. You can upload your creatives, select sites on which you want to advertise, and set a CPC you're willing to pay. This allows you to test your ad creatives, while only paying if you get a click. You can select CPM instead, but our goal here is to test at a low cost. Let's look at the *Google* process to set this up.

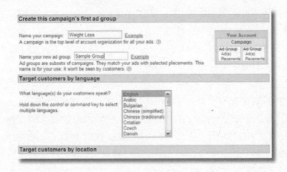

Begin your test by setting up an ad campaign. Let's use weight loss as our subject matter for our offers, and we'll set up this campaign with the name *"Weight Loss."* We can have different ad groups to separate ads out into groups by subtopic, but for now, we'll just work with one.

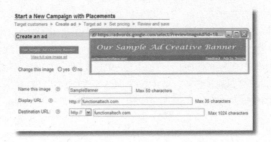

Here we're uploaded a 728 x 90 pixel leader board ad we had designed for the campaign. (I did a full size inset here so you can see it better.) It is uploaded as an image, with our ad name and landing page entered. There is an option to upload multiple ads in this screen; We'll do that as part of our test.

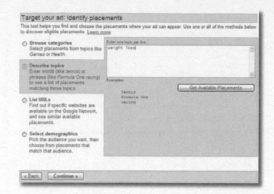

In the next step, we select specific sites for our ad placements. Instead of categories, I just entered the keywords *"weight loss."* This will pick up sites that participate in *Google*'s content network and whose subject matter is related to weight loss. We get quite a list, so I've taken three screen shots of portions of the list.

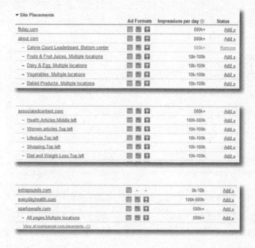

We've got lots of choices, and would want to visit these sites to see what they look like, their content, and what type of ads are currently running there. Of course, sites with the greatest number of impressions per day would have stiffer competition for ad space, and would result in a higher cost for our testing. However, we're going to elect to pay per click, so we just need to bid high enough to get the ad shown to gather data on our CTR. The icons in the center indicate what size and shape ads the site takes. Just about all of them accept leader board 728 x 90 ads, thus our selection for this demonstration.

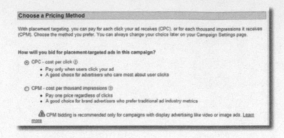

Once we've selected our sites, we can choose the pricing method. We want CPC, or cost per click, so that we only pay if there is a click on our ad. We can get the CTR data we need this way without spending a lot of money for impressions that don't generate clicks.

Because we should have uploaded multiple ad images, we'll be checking them against each other to see how each performs. We'll come out of this test with data as to whether any of the ads are working, and which ones. By selecting CPC, the next screen offers a daily budget selection, and a maximum amount to pay per click.

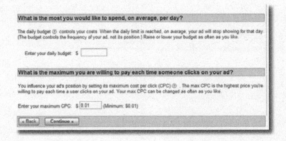

We can control our testing budget with our answers. However, you're competing with your maximum CPC bid as well. If it's too low, your ad simply will not show, or will show very infrequently, thus making our testing more difficult. So once you've entered these numbers, *Google* will give you some estimates in future screens that will help you to see how many times *Google* thinks your ads will show, and anticipates CTR based on these results.

Adjust as you go to get enough impressions for our testing of CTR for all of the ads. Remember, we're doing this to get enough information to go back and negotiate with individual sites for CPM rates and frequency caps. That doesn't mean you can't do some long-term advertising through *Google*'s content network, but taking the direct route to the sites will cut out one more middleman.

Tribalfusion.com

Tribalfusion.com is an affiliate network specializing in CPM advertising. Using a network like this speeds up the process of finding sites for your advertising. *Tribalfusion's* states that they are highly selective in choosing the sites they represent. Selection is based on high quality content. They assign sites to channels, which helps to target advertiser ads. A channel can be selected, with similar content sites, or targeting can be by site.

AD SPECIFICATIONS

Size Chart | Standard Formats| Rich Media Formats

SIZE CHART

Unit Size	Standard	Rich Media
468x60	16k	20k
728x90	20k	30k
300x250	20k	30k
336x280	20k	30k
120x600	20k	30k
160x600	20k	30k
Pop-Under	30k	40k

iFrame/JavaScript tags accepted for 3rd party serving.

The site provides guidance and third party resources for ad creative design as well. As we discussed in the advertising networks section, the network's income is based on yours. If you don't succeed, their income drops, so it's in their best interests to help you design ads that work, and then to target precisely the placement to a get great CTR.

Adbrite.com

Adbrite advertises 290 million impressions every day on more than 100,000 sites. This network places everything from text ads to full page ads on the sites they represent. It allows targeting by location, age group, and gender, as well as choosing by site categories and individual sites.

Here's what *Adbrite* says about its conversion tracking:

"Once you've got conversion tracking set up, you'll be armed with lots of rich site-level conversion data, and you can optimize your campaign and drive up conversions at your target CPA (cost per action). First, pause all

non-converting sites, and then reduce bids on sites converting above your target CPA. Increase bids on sites converting below your target CPA, since there are probably more conversions to be had. With all this in place, you should be able to increase your daily budget to drive as many conversions as possible."

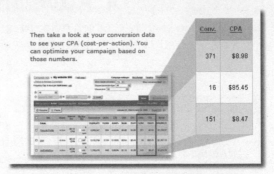

When you're new to CPM advertising, you may find that you'll get a faster start with networks like *Tribalfusion* and *Adbrite*. This takes out the individual negotiations with sites, allowing you to concentrate more on your ad creatives, offers, and multiple site selections.

Once you realize success with these networks, you can move on to individual site marketing, armed with more confidence in your ability to create the right ads for the right offers. You will also have gained CTR experience and understand which site types work best for certain products, services, and offers.

Success Story # 5 – Dwight

Using just one of Anthony's strategies, I was able to generate over $700 in a single day! In that same month I generated more than $1,600, and I was just getting started. These tools, PPC and CPM techniques, and the instruction on how to negotiate deals do really work. And being new to the business never hurt me in my negotiations when I followed Anthony's instructions.

CHAPTER 3
Social Media for Advertising

Advertising Turned Upside-Down

Enter the Internet, and the world changed forever. The printing press was big, but it can't hold a candle to *Facebook*, *MySpace* and *Twitter*. Communication has taken a step that's measured in light years. And when communication changes or evolves, marketing and advertising does the same. It's just communication for business.

Let's examine one consumer base and the ways in which we reach it traditionally, and then turn it upside-down with social media marketing. The consumer base we're referring to is the college student, busy with their lives and education. Traditionally, we:

• place notices and ads on campus bulletin boards.
• install banner ads on the fences in the sports stadiums.
• sponsor sports teams with uniforms, sports drinks and other products, purchasing endorsements for millions of dollars.
• or, perhaps a large corporation buys the stadium name.
• another corporation donates millions, hoping that students will purchase their products or services.
• ads are placed in student newspapers, on campus radio stations, and anywhere else that students might see them.

All of the above works, or it wouldn't be such a huge budget item for so many companies. But just how effective is it in relation to the expenditures? After all, exposure takes place during the busy life of a college student on campus. Rushing to and from class, socializing, and studying are activities that consume most of our target customer's time and energy. But that's the nature of these traditional methods.

Now, let's take a look at social media, *Facebook*, *MySpace*, *Twitter* and others. Advertising on these social channels is directed at the very same target, the college student. But when will they see our ads on these sites? It won't be while they're rushing to class or cheering their team to a touchdown. It won't be when they're occupied with all of the busy activities of a college student. It will be when they aren't doing anything else; they are at their computer and choose to visit the social media site without other distractions. The chances of our advertising being seen and action being taken as a result are much *greater than* with social media marketing. But there's another facet, and it's huge. While the traditional marketer is spending millions to reach thousands, we're spending thousands to reach millions.

There's the upside-down benefit of social media marketing. Advertising is only effective if it generates revenue in sales. When we can spend far less, and our reach is far greater, it's going to put a lot more money in our pockets. After all, we really do not want to narrow our target audience to just one college campus. The prospective customer base is far too small to generate the income we want. We'll hit millions of students all around the world through marketing on sites like *Facebook*, *MySpace*, and *Twitter*.

What's Happening With The Social Networks?

Twitter

At the time this is being written, the 2009 election for the leader in Iran had just been completed, with great turmoil and disputes about who really won. *The U.S. State Department* actually asked *Twitter* to postpone their planned night downtime for server maintenance to allow the millions of tweets in Iran to continue in hopes of helping to resolve the issue.

Nielsen Online reported in March 2009 that *Twitter* was growing at a rate of 1,382%! With more than 7 million unique visitors in the month of February 2009, the trend seems to be accelerating. Keep in mind that many users of *Twitter* don't access the site directly, but through third party sites like *Twhirl* and *TweetDeck*. So the numbers are even higher.

Facebook

Facebook's recent announcement that their users could get a vanity URL, one with their name in it, caused a modern-day gold rush. Millions of these URL's were signed up in the first few hours. Disputes arose, and some celebrities are filling out a special form with *Facebook* to protest the poaching of URL's for their famous names.

In the period between July 2008 and January 2009, *Facebook*'s U.S. users grew by almost 60% to more than 42 million. Virtually every age group measured is growing rapidly. Considering that *Facebook* has been around longer than *Twitter*, it's relevant that the growth in users is still strong and steady.

MySpace

In January 2009, *TechCrunch* reported that *MySpace* was still the largest social network in the U.S. The same report stated that *Facebook* was rapidly overtaking *MySpace* in users and visits. However, *MySpace*, with a younger age demographic, is still an excellent marketing media for offers that appeal to the younger set.

In the *TechCrunch* report, *MySpace* is quoted: "*In a tough economic climate, our international revenue is up 35 percent year over year and we continue to focus on those markets with the strong monetization opportunities. Additionally, MySpace continues to dominate the U.S. market–where the bulk of online advertising revenues reside–both in terms of monetization and user engagement with more than 76 million unique users and a 40% spike in engagement year over year.*"

LinkedIn

LinkedIn is a much more business-focused network, though it's still part of the social networking growth trend. One report shows that, while *Facebook* grew more than 100% last year, *LinkedIn* grew by a whopping 319%. *LinkedIn* users are, for the most part, professionals, management employees, headhunters, and the self-employed, all promoting their expertise and businesses.

Many of the large number of offers we affiliate marketers have at our disposal are technology or commodities used in business. With business owners and managers spending their time interacting on *LinkedIn*, there is opportunity there for the affiliate marketer.

As A Group – Social/Business Networks Make Sense for Us

It's easy to see that social and business networks are drawing users at a rapid pace. But that's just part of the story. These are some of the most *"sticky"* sites on the Web. On the Internet, *"stickyness"* refers to the amount of time a visitor spends on a site. If a site keeps them involved, and keeps them moving around on that site, then it is said to be sticky. These social and business networks are up on more screens for longer time periods than just about any other category of Web sites.

As affiliate marketers, we simply can't ignore marketing resources that not only have billions of page views every day, but that also keep visitors engaged for long periods of time. If your ad is on a *Facebook* page where a visitor sits for a while reading their friends' comments, there's a far better chance that your ad will be noticed, and maybe get that click you need.

Advertising on *Facebook*

Facebook makes it easy for you to design an ad, decide on placement, and whether you want CPC or CPM pricing for your advertising.

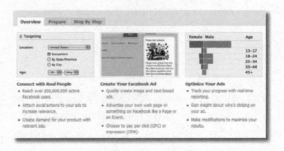

This is the first tab of the *Facebook* tutorial on advertising on the site. As with other ad networks, you target your audience, create your ad, then monitor and optimize your results.

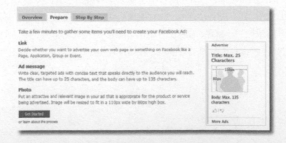

You can use up to 25 characters for a title and 135 characters in your ad text. *Facebook* will resize your image to the 180 x 80 pixels in their ads.

The next three screen shots give you an example of the simplicity of getting your ads going on *Facebook*. You get a lot of choice in targeting, and you get to set your daily budget and maximum you're willing to pay for a click.

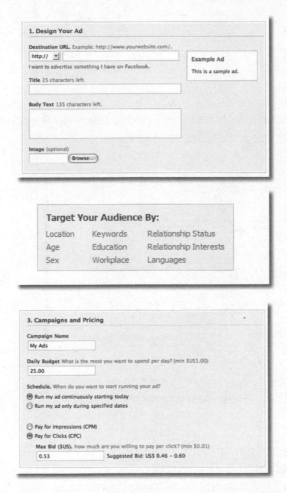

Back to our college student example. Millions of students from thousands of campuses are on *Facebook* every day. Who needs a stadium banner a few hundred might see but are not really interested in? We'll be placing our offer in front of millions, precisely when they're focused on the computer screen.

Advertising on *MySpace*

MySpace offers precise targeting of prospects by a number of criteria. As far as major groups with a common interest, they have this graphic on their home page:

When we click on the "*learn more*" link, we see how they drill down from major interests to far more focused groups.

Hyper-targets are a great term for these. We want to keep drilling down in their interest groups or age groups or location groups, until we can "*hyper-target*" the absolute best group for our offers. Here's an example of the beginning of their ad setup process:

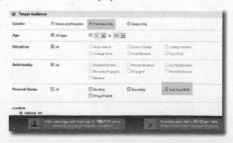

This is a cool feature. As we change our demographic criteria, the two boxes at the bottom change. Let's say that we have an offer for a weight loss product, and we decide to target females of any age who just gave birth. Two clicks, and we have our expected target audience at more than 180,000, and we can get exposure for as little as a two cents per click bid.

Advertising On *LinkedIn*

With *LinkedIn*, it's all about business, professional image, and locating professionals to hire or provide expertise. *LinkedIn*'s reaches over 35 million business professionals with an average income of $109,000. *LinkedIn* offers a text ad *"above the fold"* with targeting options. *"Above the fold"* simply means that the ad will show above the bottom of most screens, without the viewer having to scroll down to see it.

Very similar to our other ad setup steps, we devise our text for the ad; with a headline we hope will grab the attention of the site visitor. For guidance here, look back at our *Google* ad process.

Here we see how targeting works for *LinkedIn* ads. Let's say that we're going to link to the all-in-one printer category page at *Buy.com*. This would send the client, with our affiliate link, to look at a whole lot of printers. No matter which they buy, if they buy one, we get our payout. So we decided to target our ad to those who have indicated they are engaged in corporate business supplies and equipment job functions. Wow, that's a pretty narrow group, just what we need. It's narrow, but it's deep, with more than 172,000 members who will be exposed to our ad.

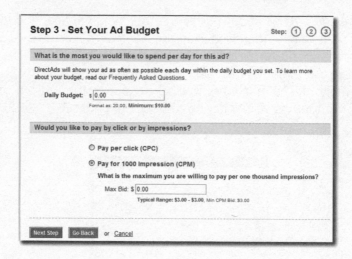

The last step is much like all of our other advertisers. We give *LinkedIn* our daily budget, and how we want to be priced, CPC or CPM.

For our printer example, we are positioning our offer to be displayed above the fold, along the right side of the *LinkedIn* pages when one of our target consumers is using the site. If you use *LinkedIn*, you know that there are various tools in the right panel that the member uses frequently. One is the questions and answers box that the user has selected to see when they log in. So your ad is positioned among their requested information boxes.

A business owner, checking their *LinkedIn* home page multiple times a day, will be a great prospect if they have a need for a printer, or maybe they want to upgrade what they have. Some vendors offer trade-in discounts for printers, so you may get some clicks by wording your ad to target trading in their old printer that's causing problems.

Twitter – The Monster in the Closet

In March 2009, *Twitter* enjoyed its third birthday. At that same time, it was reported to be the fastest growing social networking site in the world. Celebrities are adopting *Twitter* at a fast clip, with new *Twitter* users ranging from William Shatner to MC Hammer. *Twitter* accounts are advertised on television and radio, in newspapers and magazines, and even in body art tattoos. Any medium that enjoys this much interest and is growing this fast is a great platform for advertising and generating an income online.

You don't have a *Twitter* account yet? Are you just venturing into the online world of social networking? No worries. It's all so new that you can't really be very far behind the early adopters. As new as *Twitter* is, it's still a frontier, with rampant opportunity for marketers. Taking what I teach you in this book, you can immediately begin to generate online income with *Twitter*.

Twitter is Far Better than E-mail for Reaching the Masses

E-mail has been around long enough now to have become a highly-abused communication and marketing tool. You can buy expensive E-mail lists, supposedly up to date with thousands, or even millions, of names and E-mail addresses. These lists are used tens of thousands of times every day to send billions of canned messages to hundreds of billions of addresses. A great many of these addresses aren't real, or the accounts have long since been cancelled. Other addresses are going straight to the recipient's SPAM filtering, never to be seen by a human.

Let's contrast this with *Twitter*. *Twitter* is all about people joining and voluntarily communicating with others. It began as a simple way for one person to immediately, in real time, let others know what they were doing.

Twitter messages are limited to 140 characters, the same as a cell phone text message. This works well, as it is a medium where cell phones are heavily used to post via text. However, it soon became clear that just letting your extended family know that you were having corn flakes for breakfast "right now" was not where the great value was to be had from *Twitter*.

If you are in business, and you have Web sites and/or blogs with information about your products or services, you can have this information automatically posted to *Twitter* in short-burst announcements. A sale can be announced, or you just keep putting your opinions out there or your expertise on your topic, products or services. As you do this, people begin to find you, and they can follow you if they have an interest in your tweets or subject matter. These followers are how we're going to make money with *Twitter*. With multiple *Twitter* accounts, each with a niche, such as weight loss, we can tweet about weight loss products and with information on the topic. People will discover the site and follow us. They have their own followers, who will then be exposed to our tweets as well, and some of them will in turn follow us.

Think of the potential here! In a very short time, you have a great many niche market *Twitter* accounts. With methods I show you here, you can have a great deal of content AUTOMATICALLY being posted to these *Twitter* accounts without having to write most of it. As other *Twitter* users find you, they follow, and their followers follow. It's possible to build thousands, or even millions, of followers in a very short time.

Now, instead of E-mailing a list with a high percentage of dead addresses, and even more automatic spam catchers, you can just tweet to your followers, and their accounts pass that tweet along to their followers. Yes, if you post a new tweet on your weight loss account at 10 am, by 10:01 am, it's also on the home page of all of your direct followers, and on the home pages of the *Twitter* accounts of all of your followers' followers. Think of the money-making possibilities:

1. You can get paid by the click when your followers click on links in your tweets.
2. Use the tweet link to bring the visitor to your own sites and blog offer pages, or directly to your advertisers. Again, they came with an interest, and you get paid when they click again.

Remember when *Google* was new? People made millions before others caught on to the potential there. We are at the beginning of the *Twitter* phenomenon. With explosive growth, *Twitter* is on track to become larger than *Facebook* and *MySpace* very soon. Right now, there is still a huge opportunity to get in on the front end and make money before others figure it out.

Setting up a New *Twitter* Account

Setting up a free *Twitter* account is a snap. Just go to *Twitter*.com, create a user name, upload an optional image, and tell *Twitter* a little about yourself. The next image shows the main account setup tab. Consider making the image be a photo of a really attractive woman. But, you say, I'm a big, burly guy named Fred! Well Fred, if you are a shopper on the Internet, whether you're buying diet products or joining *Netflix*, think of your photo next to every tweet from your account.

Now, replace that image of you in your mind with one of an attractive woman. You may even be a handsome guy, but the fact is, women, or the perception that the seller is a woman, make selling on the Web easier and more profitable. So, since this is about money and not ego, take a trip over to *iStockPhoto.com*, where you can buy legally licensed professional images for a couple of bucks each. Statistics show that *Twitter* accounts with a woman's image get more followers, more tweet responses, and greater profits.

You'll be setting up a great many *Twitter* accounts, and I'll give you the specifics on how to do it. Each account will be *"niche specific,"* meaning one for weight loss, another for electronics, one for skin care, anti-aging, etc. The good news is that these are free accounts, and they're really fast and easy to set up for your first tweets. Here's what the main setup tab looks like:

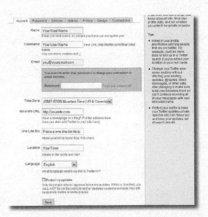

These tabs are all you need to work through, about a ten minute process, and you've got your new *Twitter* account going. A device tab allows you to set up to post to the account with a text message from your mobile phone. *"Notices"* lets you tell *Twitter* how you'd like to be notified about new followers or direct messages. *"Connections"* will be blank right now, as you use that later to connect to third party sites that add functionality to your *Twitter* experience.

Let's talk about the user name for a minute. It's a fact that you'll get more followers, which means more profits, if you use a real name here, rather than something like *"weightlossgirl"* or *"dietproductguy."* Use a real name, even if you just pick one out of a hat. People tend to want to buy from other people, and a person's name on the account will increase followers and income.

Some *Twitter* Terminology and How it Works

Follower – Someone who likes your tweets, or has an interest in what they see on your account and elects to follow you, or to get your tweets automatically as you post them. Since they have asked to get them, there is no problem with delivery as with E-mail marketing.

@reply – Let's say that you write, or auto post a tweet that mentions a weight loss product and it's linking to your offer page. If one of your followers has used the product and liked it, they could reply to your tweet by placing the @ symbol in front of your user name, as in @*yourusername*. This sends the reply to you, and also to all of your followers, and their followers.

"d" your user name – By placing a *"d"* in front of your username, a follower can send you a direct message that will not be seen by others.

Retweet – Let's say that you happen to see a tweet from a user of a product that's very positive, but they're not selling it, just saying great things about it. If it's one you market, this is a tweet you'll want to send out to your followers by re-tweeting it. See the next item for a great way to find these tweets.

Search with :) – If you are marketing a weight loss product, perhaps an acai berry product, you can do a search like this *"acai berry* **:)***"* in *Twitter* search. The smiley face only searches for tweets that sound positive about acai berry or products. Re-tweeting one of these posts adds a testimonial to your weight loss account.

There is a lot more to *Twitter*, with new tools being devised every day. As I write, there are almost 300 *Twitter* "apps." These are loosely defined as applications, sites or software that enhance the *Twitter* user experience or add functionality. For now, all you need to do is to learn what I teach you here, set up your *Twitter* accounts, get as many followers as possible, and collect your profits.

Followers are Your Customers – Build Them Aggressively

So, you've set up your *Twitter* accounts, each with a niche for products or services (I'll show you how to fill them with content later). Right now, let's see how you're going to build a list of followers that numbers in the thousands. These followers will become your customer base, clicking on your links in Tweets, going to your marketing pages, or directly visiting your advertiser offers so you can get paid.

Remember, you'll be building your followers aggressively, but every one of them also has followers. Every tweet you post will show up on your direct followers' accounts, and also on their followers' accounts. This building process can grow a lot more rapidly than you imagine. This is especially true if you employ another tool that is designed just for building followers.

Create a *Twollow.com* Account

A couple of key concepts when we're developing *Twitter* follower strategies are:

1. Reciprocal Follow – Independent research shows that approximately 40% of the people you follow will in-turn, follow you back. They are notified of a new follower, and 4 out of 10 will immediately follow you, even without looking at your account page in many cases.

2. **Auto-Follow** – One of those *Twitter* apps we talked about, in fact several, allow you to set up your account to automatically follow any new follower you get. Some of them will even send them an automated thank you for the follow. Many people use these tools, so you pick up followers when you follow, and many will be totally automatic.

Twollow.com is a service that allows you to enter keywords and phrases, automatically following any *Twitter* account that posts using these words. Let's say that you're doing that acai berry product offer, and you enter that phrase into your *Twollow* account. Or, you might go much broader, and enter *"weight loss,"* or *"diet pill,"* or *"diet product."* When someone uses the phrase in a tweet, you are automatically set up as a follower of their tweets.

You need to get outside the box with your thinking to fully appreciate the value of this concept. There are thousands, maybe tens of thousands, of posts each day that will use the acai berry phrase, or one of the others. Every single time the phrase is found on a site you're not already following, you automatically become a follower. If you're automatically following hundreds of people every other day, and 40% tend to follow back, you're building a network of followers at a rapid clip, and without any effort on your part.

Let's think back to traditional marketing for a moment. A lot of TV, radio and print marketing is designed to attract eyeballs. The more eyeballs, the greater the number of impressions, and hopefully, the more actual customers that will result. But to get those eyeballs, you're spending a fortune on ad design, production and placement, and who knows what the result might be?

Now, we're setting up a network of free *Twitter* accounts, getting followers for free, and we're reaching their followers for free. *Twollow.com's* free account is limited in the number of searches you can have, but it may suffice for your needs. Their paid accounts are not cheap, but you may want to take that step once you have some experience and get a track record for your followers and the clicks you get.

It isn't all about niche accounts with *Twitter*. Create some general accounts, without any specific niche. These are just to generate followers, so you can use keywords or phrases like *"I wish, happy, sad, I want, I love,"* etc. These are general in nature, but great for generating followers for future marketing.

The Key to *Twitter* Marketing Success is Content

"Ah!" you say, "How we get to the hard part." A couple of dozen *Twitter* accounts will need fresh new content on a regular basis. With *Twitter*, that means new posts multiple times each day for each account. Wow, what a writing nightmare! Go to a calm place, because I'm about to show you how to get new content, by the thousands of posts, every day and without any writing on your part. And this content will be specifically targeted and relevant to the niche market of each *Twitter* account.

Automated *Twitter* Content from *Google* Alerts

First, if you don't already use a *Google* product like *Gmail* or *Google* Calendar, you'll need to set up a *Google* account. It's completely free, and you can use the login you already have if you use any *Google* product. Once you've set up your account, head over to *http://google.com/alerts* to get our auto-content system up and running. If you go there first, you'll get the chance to set up your new *Google* account.

Google is not the premier search engine out there for just any reason. It has honed the Internet search function to a fine edge. There are billions of pages indexed by *Google*, and now blogs are a big part of that base of content as well. This is important because blogs are much more dynamic, with new content being published much more regularly than for static Web sites. Sometimes, just to test, I'll set up a *Google* alert for a phrase I'm about to place in a post on a blog that I've had established for a while, and it's been found by *Google*. I've seen the post pop up in my E-mail as an alert in as little as five to ten minutes! *Google* found it and sent it out via *Google* alerts very quickly.

This is the first step of our auto-content system because it is how we're going to get *Google* to go out and locate content that we want, and deliver it to us, sometimes only minutes after it's appeared on the Web.

All we have to do is to use this free service to build our alerts, starting with this screen:

First, we enter the search phrase for which we want to be alerted when *Google* locates it on the Web. Let's start with our acai berry example, entering it in the box next to *"search term."*

Leave the type as *"comprehensive,"* meaning we want *Google* to look everywhere on the Web, in Web sites, blogs, video sites, etc. The *"how often"* factor needs to be changed to *"as-it-happens,"* because we want new entries as soon as possible. One of the things that will bring you followers in droves is if they find that your *Twitter* account tweet a lot of breaking news and comments before anyone else.

Last, we choose *"feed"* as our delivery method, as it will offer you E-mail, but we want a delivery method we can use for our auto-content system. So, we want *Google* to bring us an RSS Feed that will deliver all new material, blog posts, etc. as it's found on the Web. We will use this feed in the next step to post content automatically to our *Twitter* account about weight loss.

Here's how we see that feed and copy it out for our use.

Search terms	Type	Deliver to	How often	
☐ acai berry	Comprehensive	Feed 📶 View in Google Reader	as-it-happens	edit

To see this, just right-click on the orange icon or the word *"feed"*, and copy out the URL link for the next step. In case you're not familiar with RSS and news feeds, here's a really quick explanation, so you'll know what's going on behind the scenes.

RSS Feeds

An RSS feed is created when someone subscribes to content that's being updated on a Web site or blog. Those who use them normally get their *"news feed"* delivered in a *"feed reader,"* like *Google.com/Reader*. Every time the site is posted with new content, that content is delivered as an item in the news reader for those who have subscribed. It's fast, and you get a sort of customized newspaper for topics and sites you find of interest.

Because we want a feed, *Google* has created a subscription URL link at (the orange icon). That is the link where we need to have content delivered when it is first discovered on the Web by *Google*. We'll use this feed to place the content automatically on our *Twitter* niche account for weight loss. We can do this with another *Twitter* app *Twitterfeed.com*. Go to *Twitterfeed.com* and set up your account, using the *Twitter* username and password for your *Twitter* weight loss account. You'll be asked to authenticate it, giving permission for *"Twitterfeed"* to access the account with the username and password in order to post the feed content.

We just went to the New Feed entry page, and gave our feed a title, in this case *"Acai Berry."* We paste in the RSS feed URL that we copied out of *Google* alerts.

In the *"advanced settings"* section, we set our time between checks to the shortest allowed, currently 30 minutes. We also set for up to 3 new entries in each posting cycle. Once we're done, we just click the *"create feed"* button, and our automated content feed is set up and will begin feeding our weight loss account with all new content about acai berry that *Google* finds on the Web.

Now, don't stop there. We're going to find some other key phrases for our weight loss products and do the same thing, as many times as we like. You've just become a prolific writer for the Web on many products and services related to weight loss. And you haven't written a word of your own content! Better yet, it's happening 24/7/365, even when you're fishing or sleeping.

Now Let's Make Some Money with Our *Twitter* Accounts

We now have multiple niche marketing *Twitter* accounts, and an automated system to feed them with constant updated content specifically relevant to the products and services we're marketing. Now it's just a matter of getting paid for the exposure we've created. We have two options, and we can do both:

1. We can place advertisements that pay us per click.
2. We can place links to our affiliate offers, or directly to our advertiser pages that pay us when the visitor takes the desired action.

The "Get Paid Per Click" Method

As *Twitter* grows in popularity and number of users, advertising companies grow as well. After all, with millions of avid *Twitter* users in their accounts every day, advertisers want to get their names, products and services in front of them. A bit like the affiliate networks, these *Twitter* advertising companies sign up advertisers who then state what they're willing to pay for each click to their site. Visit these sites and sign up for accounts so that you can compare them and start advertising for click money:

RevTwt at *www.RevTwt.com*

Be-a-magpie at *www.be-a-magpie.com*

Twittad.com at *www.twittad.com*

Once you have accounts at one or more of these sites, earning money will become as simple as placing their ads in your *Twitter* accounts and waiting to get paid when one of your followers, or one of your followers' followers, clicks on the ad. DO NOT post any ads until you have at least 300 followers and at least 30 updates on your *Twitter* account. You want established visibility, and the more followers you have, the more money you will make.

RevTwt is probably my favorite of the group. Right now, most of their advertisers pay around $0.05 per click on posted ads. I can easily get 3 to 5 clicks per day for each of my accounts for each ad every day it's posted. You are only allowed to post 4 ads per day per *Twitter* account, so let's run the math:

4 ads X 3 clicks X 10 accounts X $0.05 = $6.00 per day

This doesn't seem like a lot of money; however, what if you have 100 *Twitter* accounts? You could easily earn $20 per day, and that's completely automated, with you doing nothing but checking your *PayPal* account for deposits. The more accounts, the greater the income.

But that's just the number of accounts factor. What about the number of followers? Research shows that *Twitter* ads get clicked about 0.3% of the times they are shown. This means that for every 1,000 followers you have, you'll get approximately 3 clicks per ad showing. That's where I got the 3 clicks in the example calculation above. Now, let's say you have 10,000 followers on sites where your ad will appear. The math changes a lot:

4 ads X 30 clicks X 10 accounts X $0.05 = $60.00 per day

Now we're talking serious money from a totally automated process that just keeps on working for us 24/7/365 in every corner of the planet. More advertisers and vendors are coming online every day, so keep up with them. As competition gets tougher, there will be higher offers for click payments. Check the math above; if we're getting $0.07/click instead of a nickel, we now earn $84 every day.

Taking the Pay per Click Model to the Next Level

You've set up multiple *Twitter* niche accounts, built systems to increase your followers at a rapid rate, and have ads running which makes you a nice daily income. That is great, but there's a way to make even more money, and it's just as automated, with no time or effort on your part once it's set up. *RevTwt.com*, and some others, offer a 20% *"residual"* income to you from money paid to those you send to their network. In other words, if you refer someone to *RevTwt*, and they set up an account and run ads, you'll receive 20% of what *RevTwt* gets paid on an ongoing basis.

Of course this idea appeals to you, but how do you get enough people to sign up to make it an automated profit machine? First sign up for an account at *TweetLater.com*, it's free. Once you have your account and it's connected to your *Twitter*, you can set it up to send an automated reply to all new followers. You place your referral link from *RevTwt* into a message something like one of these:

**"You can earn money with Twitter
[RevTwt referrallinkhere]."**

OR

**"Your Twitter account can make money!
[RevTwt referrallinkhere]"**

So you've taken all of the steps in our *Twitter* money-making process, and you're building followers at a rapid rate. Each new follower now receives an automated reply like one of these, and the referral link is there to click. Many will click on it out of curiosity, if for no other reason. So how does this look for income generation?

Your new follower generation system is cranking on multiple *Twitter* accounts. You're getting 1,000 new followers every day. Let's say that only one in five, or 20%, of them actually click on the referral link in the automated reply. And let's say that half of those sign up, and they only earn $0.10 a day each. Here is your income potential:

Day 1: 1,000 followers, with 200 clicking & 100 signing up = $2.00/day

Day 2: $3

Day 3: $4

It's easy to see that this income builds all by itself, and we based it on a pretty low income for each of our referrals. The better they do, the more we'll see in income, and it will grow every day. It's on auto-pilot, and we're just checking our cash inflow in our *PayPal* account.

The "Affiliate Marketing Income" Method

Now that you've set up all of these niche *Twitter* accounts are feeding them with automated relevant content, and are building a huge follower base, it's time to earn a lot more money by promoting your own affiliate offers with *Twitter* posts. Through your affiliate networks, you have hundreds of offers in numerous vertical markets from which to choose. Using our weight loss *Twitter* account as an example, we can check out a large number of affiliate offers related to diet, health and weight loss.

It's easy to choose offers, place the affiliate link in the tweet, and post it to your *Twitter*. With 140 characters, you're thinking like a *Google* PPC ad, in that you have limited space in which to generate interest. But it doesn't have to look like an advertisement. It can take the form of a testimonial, such as *"I just tried XXXXX, and it's tasty and I'm losing weight!"* The product name can be the affiliate link. There are a number of ways you can approach running your affiliate link ads as tweets.

Using your *Tweetlater.com* account, you can have prescheduled tweets sent to your entire follower base instantly. Let's take that 0.3% click-through ratio from our previous calculation as an example. We're promoting a free sample offer of a weight loss product, a pill or other food additive. Our advertiser will pay us $2.00 for every sign up we send them for the free trial, as their experience shows that they'll convert a high percentage of these customers to a buyer once they have their contact information.

We have 10,000 followers of our weight loss *Twitter*. We run our ad, with a link to the advertiser's free trial pitch and sign up page. With a 0.3% click rate from *Twitter*, we'll get 30 clicks through to the offer page. Since it's a free trial, with no money up front, we can expect a high conversion rate. If half of the people accept the free trial:

10,000 see the ad & 30 click through, so 30/2 = 15 trials X $2.00 = $30

Then, we try this with a different product offer, and another, and so on, forever. We just made $30 by typing a quick 140 character ad and hitting the *"Enter"* key to post it. Saving the ad, and running it again next week or next month, we can likely do equally well. Many people didn't see the first ad, but will see it this second time. When an ad converts well, perhaps that affiliate advertiser has another offer that we can try next time with the same ad–say a half price first order that pays us $6 instead of the $2 for the free trial. Now we're talking $90 for that one ad post.

Once you've set up a couple of dozen niche *Twitter* accounts and you're working with hundreds of affiliate links, your income will swell. You won't become a billionaire this way, but it's an easy, automated way to generate regular cash flow with *Twitter*.

CHAPTER 4
Internet Article Advertising

With billions of pages of text on the Web, you'd think that adding more would be just one drop into deep well, never to be seen again. That's not the case. It's all about relevance and linking, with the search engines able to find just about anything they want from their search phrase and your copy. There's yet another way to market on the Web, and that's through article or *"blog post marketing."*

Some of this marketing is free, and some costs money, but most of it falls into these two types:

- writing articles for sites which aggregate them by subject matter and author.
- pay per post to get your sites promoted.

There are a lot of sites out there that make an income from running ads. I'll give you a brief rundown on some of them here. The premise is that you can write an article for the site, and they run it, selling advertising as the article is viewed. Some even share the revenue with the author, but it's usually not enough to get excited about. We're interested in getting our offer sites promoted via these articles.

Ezinearticles.com

This site syndicates articles. Experts write in their areas of knowledge, then publishers use these articles in newsletters, and searchers are able to find them. *Why should you submit your best quality original articles to EzineArticles.com?*

Because you'll get a chance to receive a massive increase in exposure, a boost in credibility and you'll be able to include a short blurb about yourself, your business and your Web site in your resource box located directly below your article body that delivers pre-qualified visitors back to your Web site. That is what we are interested in getting our offer site link into the article, and getting clicks to the site from the article.

AssociatedContent.com

This is a site that takes your article submissions and even offers to share some of the revenue with you when your article pages are viewed. They don't get enough page views for you to be concerned with income, but it's yet another free resource for getting content out there that links back to your offer sites.

GoArticles.com

This site takes articles that aren't promoting a product, but you can link out to a site. So you can write an informative article about weight loss and health considerations, linking to your offer page that has some of the same type of content.

ArticleDashboard.com

From their submission guidelines page: *"**No affiliate links!** - The articles that you submit to Article Dashboard should not contain affiliate links. It is acceptable, however, to mention the URL's of helpful sites or your own Web site which redirects to the recommended affiliate product."*

ArticleBiz.com

This site allows you to enter a URL link in a special resource box below each article.

There are many more, and you can locate them with a *Google* search on *"article submission sites,"* or something similar. The thing to remember (we'll talk about this more in the SEO chapter) is that search engines give you better page rank based on links back to your site. So, every time you place an article with a link to one of your affiliate marketing sites, you're helping your rankings with the search engines.

Hiring Writers for Articles

In the *"Platforms and Tools"* chapter, I'll go into detail about how to affordably hire writers to create content for these article sites. You'll learn how to locate writers on freelance sites like *Elance.com* and *Guru.com*, how to set up your projects for bids, and how to select a bidding writer and get what you want at the price you have in your budget. You'll be surprised how inexpensively these people will write for you.

Pay Per Post

Related to hiring writers is the PPP (*"Pay per Post"*) concept. You pay to have your sites and offers specifically mentioned on blogs and Web sites by those who offer their services through a site just for this type of promotional writing. At *payperpost.com*, you can see how this works.

The *"Pay Per Post"* **Marketplace** – Here you place your site or offer as an opportunity. You tell the site and the bloggers what you are promoting, and how you'd like it promoted and written about. You can also require that a relevant image go with the blog post. The bloggers, or *"posties"* as they call them, look at your opportunity and decide if it's something they want to write about, and create their post. The post is reviewed by the site, and if it meets requirements, they are paid out of funds you've deposited in your advertising account.

"Pay Per Post" **Direct** – This is a more focused approach. Let's say that in your weight loss research you come across a blog that has a lot of really great information, well-written, and touching on products for which you have offers. You also see that they are a member blogger, or *"postie"* with PPP, because they have a special widget, or box on their blog that lets you know this. You can click on that widget and negotiate directly with that blogger to promote your offers. There is a transaction fee through PPP for handling the payment.

It's not hard to see that you can closely focus your offers to blogs read by your target consumer. You can get traffic statistics for the blog, and negotiate the placement of a much focused ad right next to a positive blog post about the product.

We're back again to SEO. This is yet another link to one of your affiliate marketing sites, and one that's very relevant to the product or service you're marketing there. The blog reader is one interested in the topic and product, or they wouldn't be there. The blogger has built up their visitor statistics by consistently writing about "weight loss" and health topics, so they have a level of trust built up over time with their visitors. What better place to advertise your offer of a related product?

CHAPTER 5
SEO, Search Engine Optimization & Free Marketing

SEO – The Free Search Engine Strategy

We spent a large part of this section of the book explaining PPC marketing, and CPM marketing. That's because they are the fastest and most targeted way to reach your audience and start generating income right away. But, you're not getting into this business for the short haul. As it will be a major source of income for you, you'll want to stay with it.

Now, you can get started with a bang and have immediate profitable operations by using PPC and CPM to get the right visitors to the right landing pages to click to your advertisers and get you paid. And you'll always be doing PPC and CPM. What if, over time, you could spend less for PPC and CPM, while increasing your visitors and income? That's what SEO is all about. It isn't fast, and it won't create miracles in weeks, more like months or years. But if you keep SEO in your plan, site design, and content writing, you'll find that you can cut your PPC and CPM budgets in the future because your visitors will be coming from free links instead of paid links.

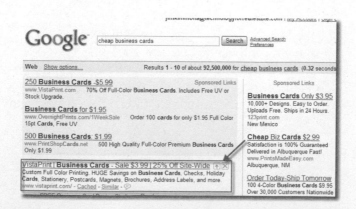

The SERP above, for the search on cheap business cards, has the common three top PPC results, with other PPC results down the right side. But the one I've boxed in red is a free ad. It's there because of the ranking *Google*'s given it over time for relevance and information about cheap business cards.

That ad is probably getting as many or more clicks than the paid ad above it, but they're not paying a dime for it. The ad above it may be spending hundreds of dollars every month. I'm not saying that you'll ever be able to take that position away from this company, but you might for your offer and certain keywords. And guess what? I have heard people say that they will not click on the paid ads. Granted, that's a minority viewpoint, but one that's valid. These people understand the system, and they know which ads are the paid ads. They believe that they can get more relevant information from an ad that had to compete for position based on content rather than budget.

Many advertisers who manage to get free positions in the top five, and even some in the top 10 for first page, make a great deal of money from clicks. If we're creating content and landing pages anyway, and we're trying to make them relevant for a better PPC ad quality score from *Google*, *Yahoo* or *MSN*, would we not want extra income free by getting into the top five or ten free results? It's not something that needs to be an obsession, but it's something to keep in mind in all of your activities related to affiliate marketing. Better position in the free results comes from:

- optimizing a Web or landing page for no more than two or three key phrases
- using the key phrases in one or more of these places:
  - the title of the page
  - bold
  - sub-headings or bullets
  - the first sentence or near the beginning
  - the last sentence or near the end
- write articles elsewhere that link back to the page with one of the targeted key phrases in the link text in the article
- get your page mentioned and linked to from as many relevant sites and blogs as possible over time

None of this is rocket science and we're already doing some of it for our PPC landing pages and article marketing anyway so, we're not really looking at a lot of extra work here. Keeping these strategies and techniques in mind when building Web pages, writing blog posts, and placing articles.

Remember, this isn't a speedy process; results take months to years, but it works. If you know you're going to be doing this a few years from now, your content will be out there for a long time, so why not just put it out there search engine optimized in the first place? Part of the search engine's ranking criteria is site age as well, so time is on your side.

Other Free Marketing Tools and Strategies

Link from Absolutely EVERYWHERE

You're building profiles for *Facebook*, *LinkedIn*, *MySpace*, *Twitter*, and any other networking Web sites you can find. You don't even have to participate. If it's free, and it lets you enter a link to your marketing, then fill in the profile and place as many links as they'll allow.

Post classifieds to *CraigsList* with links to your specific offers or to pages of multiple offers. Use any other free classified site that you can find to do the same thing. Remember, they're there to sell things. The fact that you are linking the visitor to the vendor for stuff doesn't matter. If they're looking for it, then put an ad in there about it.

Use the Social and Business Networks Aggressively

I just mentioned the networks, but you're not just looking for a place where they invite you to place a link, such as in your profile. You're also going to be chatting with others on the networks, and you can place links in those posts as well. Watch for questions that lead to an answer with an offer link. *LinkedIn,* for example, gives you many opportunities with their structured question and answer section.

Send your *Twitter* feeds to the networks that allow it. Do the same with your blog RSS feeds. Your posts will show up on your profile pages, and you'll get clicks and money from this exposure, plus some search engine optimization help as well.

Get Active in the Blogging Community with Comments & Trackbacks

A phrase created when blogging hit the mainstream is *"link love."* Because blogging is a social and commentary style of communication, it breeds interaction between bloggers. You will blog about a topic that is the same as many others. There is an opportunity for you to quote (not copy extensively) content from their blog posts that are relevant to what you're writing about. When you do this, it results in a *"trackback"* to their site that lets them know that you mentioned them and linked to their site. Many bloggers consider it common courtesy to return the favor.

Here's what one looks like under a post in a real estate blog:

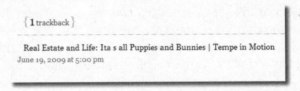

{ 1 trackback }

Real Estate and Life: Ita s all Puppies and Bunnies | Tempe in Motion
June 19, 2009 at 5:00 pm

This is an automatic function with *WordPress* and other blogs, so they don't have to do anything for your trackback to show up. This is a simple way to create your own one-way link back to your site from a popular blog. The value of these links back are based on the popularity of the blog they're coming from.

Commenting is the other way to get your link in a blog, and create a conversation. Use *Google* alerts to send you an E-mail or RSS feed notices of blog posts on topics of interest, or on those you blog about for your best offer payouts. Give them a look if the title is enticing, and write a short comment, even if it's only that you liked the post and why. This gives you the opportunity to set your link to your offer page.

Bringing Advertising All Together

This has been a really big section, and rightly so. You can have beautiful Web sites and informative blogs, great SEO, and high payout offers on great landing pages. But if you don't get enough visitors in a reasonable period of time, it's not going to be the profit generator you hoped for.

I've given you the tools, and some specific, little-known strategies to pull maximum visitors to your sites for maximum income.

PPC and CPM Advertising

Use what I've given you here to pay for highly targeted traffic to your sites, landing pages and offers. This is without a doubt the fastest and most effective way to get the right visitor to the right offer for that click that gets you paid.

The Social and Business Networks

You can pay for advertising on *Facebook*, *MySpace* and *LinkedIn* as well. Your ad can be targeted to specific groups; by gender, age or occupation. Again, you're able to bring the visitor to your site who is most likely to take the action you need for your payout.

You have an awesome tutorial on how to make money with *Twitter* in two ways, and how to build a follower bases for each of your niche markets. *Twitter* is so new, and growing so fast, what I've shown you here is not known by most users.

Article and *"Pay per Post"* Marketing

I've given you the information and resources you need to place articles on sites all around the Web, linking back to your sites, offers and landing pages. It's almost all free, and these links back have SEO value as well.

SEO and Free Marketing Tools

Over time, the tips I've given you here will bring more traffic to your sites at a lower overall cost. Free traffic is always preferable to paying for it, and you profit margins rise dramatically.

Success Story # 6 – Jacques

"My name is Jacques, I came to the United States in 1985 to seek a better life. I went to school and I got a degree in business administration. I have always loved business; my dream was always to run my own business. Besides my 9 to 5 job as a social worker, I am always in pursuit of a successful investment. I tried a lot of other programs until I found the affiliate marketing system, and yes, it works. It really changed my life. There is no need to travel, no product to sell, and you don't have to deal with people.

Anyone can go online during their leisure time and browse the Internet and buy my products, even when I am sleeping. The best technique that helped me to be successful in this program is word of mouth advertising. For example, I advised my co-workers to visit my Web site, at church I asked my brothers and sisters to do the same. I called family members, friends, people that I know anywhere in the United States, and told them about my online business, and asked them to tell friends about it also. I did some online advertising, and I have my business card posted in a lot of stores.

Since I am a very positive person, my expectation is really high concerning the affiliate program. I expect to make more money than I could make with my regular job. My first check with the affiliate program was over $2,000.00, and I made it in less than 3 weeks! I thank Anthony for his help and support, and as my mentor, and teacher, I know he will continue to work and invest in me until I become just like him."

In the next section, we will explain the platforms for your affiliate marketing and the tools to build on these platforms.

SECTION IV
MARKETING PLATFORMS AND THE TOOLS TO BUILD & MANAGE THEM

CHAPTER 1
Web sites

What Works With Web sites

Web sites are one of the best ways to generate fast income in affiliate marketing. The typical Web site is a shopping mall of sorts, with all of your affiliate offers there. The visitor, who may have arrived on a weight loss search, can also shop for electronics, books, or anything else you place on the site.

You will also get repeat traffic once a visitor realizes what's available at the site. The downside is that this is less focused shopping, so your CTR will be somewhat less, as they're likely not there on a mission to locate one product that's important to them right now.

The Web site is a great platform for the beginner, as they can get a lot of help in getting one up, including template sites and turnkey affiliate marketing sites. With a template or turnkey site, the beginner can be online and generating clicks in days.

Almost all offers and products or services work well on this type of Web site. Whether it's weight loss, anti-aging, *as seen on TV,* or others, they'll all work well on a Web site platform.

Hosting – The Home for Your Web site

Web sites are a little like home sites. As home sites are plots of land in a subdivided larger parcel, Web sites are portions of a Web server where each is stored with its own main URL ("*Uniform Resource Locator*") that tells the browser precisely where the Web site is on the vast network of the Internet. Many Web servers are connected to form the Internet.

I want to make clear that I'm giving you detailed information about each tool and resource necessary for doing your own Web site design, management, and content development. This doesn't mean you must do it all, or even most of it. I'll also give you sources to get template sites where you just enter your content, and you don't have to worry about hosting or design. Finally, I'll give you a turnkey solution that is set up for affiliate marketing with vendors and offers in place and managed for you.

This is excellent information that will help you evaluate services and Web site hosting and design offers. But you can do as little or as much as you want. Read the detail, use it in your decision-making, but remember that you can get up and running with an affiliate marketing Web site with little of your time and effort.

Space and Bandwidth

There are two things you're paying for when you set up a hosting account. It will only be one monthly or annual cost, but the space your Web site uses, or its plot size as with land, is one thing. The other is *"bandwidth"* or the number of bytes of data downloaded by your visitors in a certain period of time. First, the cost of space on the Web has steadily decreased over time, so it's a really low cost item, and generally you will be getting plenty of space from your hosting provider for your Web site to sit in.

However, you'll also want to compare hosting providers based on the bandwidth allowed for your site. Every time a site visitor asks to see a page, there is a certain amount of data that is sent to their browser, or downloaded to them. The more visitors, and the more pages they view, the greater the bandwidth your site is using. Image heavy sites use more, as they are much larger in byte size than text files. Since we use a lot of product images, bandwidth is important.

As time goes by, more and more hosting providers are responding to competition by providing unlimited space and bandwidth for some of their accounts. If that's what you find at a hosting provider's site, then they could be a great choice. This is true of some who offer unlimited space and bandwidth for as little as $9.95 per month. Some also offer an unlimited number of Web sites on the account as well. This allows you to have a separate site for each product type or break them out in any way you wish. This requires a quick explanation of *"shared"* and *"dedicated"* hosting.

Shared Hosting

Your site shares an IP address (example: 163.28.147) with other sites. It is more economical for the host, and you get a much lower price for your site space and hosting. Generally, this works fine for most of us as long as their servers and facilities are top notch. However, at times, something someone else does to blow up their site that's sharing an IP with you can cause your site problems as well.

Dedicated Hosting

"Dedicated hosting" is more expensive, because you're getting your own IP address. This is a choice you may make solely based on the cost involved.

Let's talk about *"uptime guarantees"* and hosting providers. Just about all of them guarantee that your site will be up, without problems, for 99% of the time. The problem is, this is easy to say, but not always what is delivered. They generally give you some kind of a credit if your site is down more, but a one month credit of $9.95 isn't going to make up for the revenue you lose if your site is down for hours.

Go to *Twitter* and *Google* and do searches on the hosting provider's site name with downtime or complaints in your search. You can also use *Twitter*'s advanced search with a frown face to get posts that have negative wording about that host, as in a search for *"hostprovider* **:(**" This quick bit of research could turn up complaints of excessive downtime and send you to another hosting provider before you have a huge Web presence on their servers with a gigantic cost in time and money to move it later.

E-mail & Hosting Providers

All of the hosting providers offer a certain number of E-mail addresses with their hosting accounts. As costs have dropped, most are providing several hundred E-mail addresses, so you'll likely not have a need that exceeds what they provide off-the-shelf. Numerous E-mail addresses with a domain are helpful in tracking response to offers, as you can provide links in sites and E-mails that represent different offers or ad text. Then you can track responses by the "*From*" address to see what is working best for you.

Some Hosting Providers to Check Out

I receive no commission in listing these sites, so I strongly recommend that you research thoroughly before making decisions about hosting. Here are a few of the hosting providers that have been in the Web news lately due to their growth.

Hostgator.com

Hostgator.com (*www.hostgator.com*) is a hosting provider advertises that they host almost 2 million sites, and have a support staff of 200. From their site:

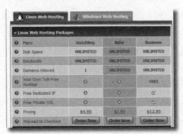

BlueHost.com

BlueHost (*www.bluehost.com*)is very similar to *HostGator* in that their offerings and guarantees of unlimited space and bandwidth and costs as low as $6.95 per month.

Here is a partial feature list from their site.

FEATURES INCLUDED / ALL ACCOUNTS	INCLUDED
Disk Storage (NOW MORE!)	Unlimited
Host *UNLIMITED* Domains (WOW!)	✓
Free Drag and Drop Site Builder (NEW!)	✓
Free Domain Name	✓
Support International Domain Names	✓
POP3/POP3 Secure Email Support	2,500
IMAP/Secure IMAP Email Support	2,500
3 Different Web Based Email Solutions	✓
Forwarding Email Accounts	Unlimited
Email Autoresponder	Unlimited
Gigs of Site Transfer (NOW MORE!)	Unlimited
Add-on Domains	Unlimited
Parked Domains	Unlimited
Subdomains	Unlimited
Additional FTP Accounts	1,000

Rackspace.com

Rackspace *(www.rakspace.com),* is a more sophisticated solution, with more support, design help and features that tie in to larger corporate E-mail and database requirements, & for very large site structures. From their site:

Domain Names

Many hosting providers will give you a certain number of free domain name registrations as part of their service, but you'll likely end up purchasing a great number of domains, so you'll want less expensive resources, and you'll want to be able to manage them without a lot of hassle.

What is a Domain Name?

A *"domain name"* is the language equivalent to an IP address. People don't want to type in 158.184.25.6 to find a Web site of interest. Thus, we have domain names like *http://yoursite.com* to be friendlier. You purchase the right to a domain name for a specific period of time. If you don't renew this right at the end of that time, the domain name goes back on the market and it no longer directs to your site.

A domain name points to a certain URL or IP address. It's just a more memorable and marketable way to bring the visitor, not to mention much easier to talk about. So you'll be buying a lot of domain names with word combinations that indicate the content of your offer site or even a certain page. Because you can point a domain name at any page on the Internet, you can have one site with a main domain name of something like *"exclusiveoffers.com,"* while you may have a dozen other domain names pointing to offer pages at that site.   Example: One of the pages reviews weight loss offers. You might buy a domain name like *"myreviewsonweightloss.com,"* and point it at that one page.

Domain Name Registrars

The registrar or provider of the domain name is where you sign up and purchase it. There are different costs, but it's getting a lot less expensive than it used to be. Using sites like *GoDaddy.com* or *Yahoo.com*, you can get a domain name for a year for around $10. You can get discounts for multiple years, and also for a large number of domains.

Remember that this can be independent of your hosting provider if you want it to be. You can host your site one place, and buy domain names somewhere else, just pointing them to where you want the visitor to end up when they use it.

Web site Structure & Design

When we go into blogs later, and I'll give you a rundown of the differences in structure, display and content management for blogs versus Web sites. Right now, let's simply consider a Web site as a more static rendition of your content on the Internet. It will be changed and have new content added infrequently, though in our affiliate marketing, we'll be changing offers and links somewhat regularly.

What we find with a Web site is that the way elements display on a page is controlled by the HTML in the background, and most of today's Web sites use tables, with rows and columns, to get content to display where they want it on the screen.

WYSIWYG - *What You See Is What You Get*

WYSIWYG is the acronym for "*What You See Is What You Get*." This means that when you're designing a Web page, you are looking at the results of your work as it will display on your page, rather than at a bunch of HTML code.

Using WYSIWYG and tables, you can design a Web page and place elements around the screen where you want them, much as using tables in your word processor.

Button	Button	Button	Button	Button
	Image		Image	
Text		Text		Text

The rows and columns in the table above is a simple rendition. If formatted to take up the entire screen size you're designing for, these cells would allow you to place content around the screen where you want it to show up. There is a lot of design software out there that lets you set up Web pages with WYSIWYG. If you're one who wants to save money, or you just like the challenge and control of designing your own Web pages, then you might look into some of this software, and find more with a search on *"WYSIWYG Web design software."*

Coffee Cup Web Design Software

One consumer research site bills this as near the top of the list for beginners at site design. You can get a free trial download, with pricing based on features and packages you choose.

Adobe Dreamweaver

This is considered the top end of Web design software, and at $399 list without any discounts, it's priced for the serious Web site developer. However, it will bring just about every feature you see in any Web site into your design toolbox. The tradeoff, besides cost, is the learning curve is much steeper than other packages.

There are many more, but these two examples give you a comparison of the lower cost, easier learning curve of *Coffee Cup* with the high end, very powerful and feature rich, *Dreamweaver* software. Either way, you might want to think about where your time is better spent. Do you want to be setting up money-making offer pages without the time involved in site design? If so, then one of the solutions I'll show you next is a better choice.

Paying a Freelancer for Site Construction

You have another option that can get you a custom Web site designed to your specifications and with the look you desire. It's hiring a Web design freelancer to produce it from your instructions. Later in this chapter, you'll get instructions for using the top two freelance sites for Web design and content writing. For now, just know that one of your Web site design options is to have it produced for you from scratch by a Web design professional on a project bid basis.

Template Sites for Affiliate Marketers

Another approach to getting your marketing up faster and with a lot less Web design and HTML knowledge on your part are template sites for affiliate marketing. Template sites are pre-designed with the look and features needed for a specific purpose. A real estate template site would have pages designed to display homes. An affiliate marketing template site would have product offer page designs, allowing you to just drop in your images, text and offer links.

There are thousands of choices in low-cost templates for an affiliate marketing site. Just one site, *www.templatemonster.com*, shows more than 2,000 templates using the keyword search *"affiliate marketing."* Here's a sample of a page from the site with this search:

Notice that, though you can buy an off-the-shelf template for under $100, there are options to have one made unique for your needs. Of course, the price is considerably higher. And you'll still have to enter all of your offers, images, and text, as this is just to get a unique look for your site, not content.

Before you pay a few thousand dollars to do the back-and-forth work necessary to get a unique design, make sure to read about my turnkey sites at *www.affiliatemarketing.com* to see how just a little bit more money can get you an affiliate marketing site with hundreds of offers already set up, and they'll be maintained for you as well.

Content for Your Web sites

You'll be writing short product descriptions or using those provided from your advertisers for products and offers. However, I stressed the importance of relevant landing page text in the PPC, CPM and SEO chapters earlier. You will need a lot of text written to provide the right information, and in some cases to pre-sell the customer, when they arrive at your sites. Remember that the search engines also look at the text and its relevance on your landing pages in giving you a quality rating to lower your CPC's and move you up in results, increasing your profits. You can write all of this yourself *if:*

- you have the time
- you have some writing skills
- your grammar is good
- you can use spell check and WILL
- you have SEO writing principles down

If all of these aren't true for you, you may want to pay for some writing. As other Internet costs have come down, so has the cost of professional writing using freelance writing sites. These are sites that bring together writers, Web site designers and other freelance professionals, matching them to projects that are placed for bid. I mentioned these sites as a resource for someone to bid your Web site construction, and they're excellent for getting good writing for your sites and blogs as well.

Guru.com and *Elance.com*

These are two very large and popular freelance Web sites, and they are very similar in how they work. I'll outline the main points and how you would use them, and the procedures, cautions and tips which are common to both. First, remember that you're the employer in this situation, and you have a right to expect to receive the site design or writing that you need, and when you need it. Second, pay attention to the hints and cautions here, as you can shoot yourself in the foot if you don't do a good job of project planning, description and bid evaluation.

Employers & Providers

These sites match people like you with a *"provider"* who is willing to provide site design or writing that you'll need for your Web sites for a fee. There are two distinct portions of the site; one for providers logging in to search for work, and the other for employers to post projects and search for providers with the skill set they need. Providers pay a fee to have access to all projects. Usually, the employer isn't charged to post projects, as they're bringing in the work that funds the process. The site gets a percentage of all jobs billed. There are some fees to employers that are a small percentage of the project amount, but you're not paying just to post up a project.

Creating Your Project Description

I can't stress enough the importance of making a plan, setting your plan down on paper, and communicating your project clearly in the description on the site. The vast majority of disputes between employers and providers are due to a misunderstanding of what the employer expected, and thus the delivery of something different by the provider. There are feedback procedures to report your experience with a provider, so they are concerned with how you liked their work. They don't want poor feedback on the site, as it could cost them future projects. However, the feedback sword is double-edged. Providers also rate their experience with employers, so you want to be clear, businesslike, and honest in your dealings.

Post Projects and Accept Bids

Whether its Web site design or writing content, you'll be posting your project, with a selected budget range, and a clear and detailed description of what you want. Providers will be checking their project boards for possible work and they'll locate your project if it's in their area of expertise. They will then decide on whether to bid your project or not. Some of your considerations and theirs include:

- **Your posted budget.** If it's unrealistically low, you'll get few bids, and they may be from providers that will not produce the quality you expect. You can elect "unknown or will not disclose" options for your budget if that's the case.

- **Your project description & requirements.** This is critical, as you don't want someone bidding who doesn't fully understand what you want. Be clear, with information like the number of Web pages they'll be designing for you, for example. You'll want to tell the designer an approximate number of images and words per page if they're writing content. If possible, attach example documents to the project for the provider to examine. This works well later, after you've hired others and gotten good work. A poor or vague project description will, at best, get you a lot of clarifying questions, and at worst, cause good providers to skip your project completely.

- **Evaluate the bidders and the bids.** Once you have bids, you can check the feedback, expertise, work examples, and other experience and quality factors for each bidder. Both *Elance* and *Guru* have profiles for providers with examples of previous work. You can also require that they attach examples of similar project work with their bids. LOW bid is usually not your goal at this step. With a great many foreign bidders from India, China and other countries, you'll want to be sure of their location, and whether you can communicate with them to produce quality product with American style language for your site visitors.

- **Ask for more info if you need it.** Both sites have message boards for communication before and after bid selection. If you're not sure a bidder has bid with a full understanding of your needs, just send them a message so they can address your concern.

- **Use their escrow systems for payment.** Both sites have payment systems designed to protect both the employer and the provider in the process. If you choose to use their escrow systems, you'll be placing a portion of the payment into escrow at the beginning of the project. This assures the provider that the money is available when they deliver the product to you. However, your protection is the ability to refuse the release of escrow if you're not satisfied with the delivered content or product.

- **Don't test the water too much.** Both of these sites show the provider the ratio of projects you place for bids to those you actually go forward with. Placing a lot of projects that you let expire un-awarded will be obvious, and some providers will avoid bidding your jobs. Also, if this goes too far, the site will penalize you.

- **For writing jobs, word count works best.** Good writers, especially those with a lot of knowledge about niche topics, will not want to work by the hour. Their knowledge and writing skills mean that they can turn out content quickly. So, they do not want to go to the trouble of reporting time to you, and getting less for their efforts as well. It's better to get bids by the word, or by the page. However, if it's by the page, be sure to define the font, as *Arial* 12 pt and *Times New Roman* 12 pt will result in a significant word per page difference.

E-mail To Support Your Web site Marketing

Once your Web sites are up and generating site visitors, you'll be doing various things to get an E-mail address from your visitors so that you can market other offers to them later.

- Offering special reports for E-mail delivery
- Special offers and discounts if they give you their E-mail address
- Capturing E-mail addresses from *Twitter*, *Facebook*, *MySpace*, *LinkedIn* and other sites.

You'll want to gather as many of these E-mail addresses as possible, but in a way that is legal and clear to your site visitors. Follow the *Federal CANSPAM Act*, which is a simple law, really. It is designed to avoid SPAMming and give your E-mail recipients a clear method to ask to be removed from your lists. If you don't do this for any other reason, there's a selfish one as well. Almost all E-mail systems now have an easy button for their user to designate an E-mail as SPAM. Having too many people doing this can get your IP or provider banned from that service. So, follow the rules for your own good.

Next, I want to be sure that you understand the difference between an auto-responder and *"drip"* E-mail. Though they can be the same, when you're evaluating E-mail service providers for your marketing, be sure that you know if they're only doing auto-response, or if they're doing true "drip E-mail."

Auto-response E-mail – This is, in the pure state, a single event response. Someone sees a button on your Web site to request a special report, and they click on it, sending you an E-mail which gets you their E-mail address. The auto-response is an automatic E-mail back to them with the report in the E-mail, as an attachment, or as a link to the report on the Web. You then use their E-mail in other marketing.

Limited drip E-mail – Though the term "drip E-mail" is used for both limited and full drip E-mail, it is not the same. This version of drip E-mail will allow you to enter a recipient's E-mail address and have a series of pre-written E-mails delivered to them on a time-release basis. However, if you start this type of drip E-mail campaign with 20 recipients, and the third of ten E-mails has just been sent, entering a new recipient into the list will start them on the fourth E-mail, not at the beginning.

Full drip E-mail – This is the same timed series of E-mails, but the system you're using will take in a new address, know that it's new, and start that recipient on the first E-mail in the series. Every recipient always gets every E-mail.

You'll use one or more of these E-mail systems in your marketing, depending on the goal of a campaign and other factors. However, the overall result should be more business for you because you're able to follow up with people who bought before or expressed interest, marketing future offers to them.

Example: You advertise a free weight loss report on your site that compares different products. When requested, your auto-responder sends them the report, with links to the products in it (your affiliate payout links). You place their E-mail address into your marketing campaigns, one of which is a manual release when you have a new report, and another of which might be a drip series of four E-mails, each featuring a new product not in the original report.

You can see that we're building a repeat business structure, marketing more products and related offers to those we know have an interest, and possibly have purchased before. The value of a clean and current list of prospects grouped by their interests is huge. That's why selling E-mail lists is a big industry. Don't sell yours, but do appreciate its value to your future business and profits.

AWeber

AWeber (www.aWeber.com) is one of my favorite services for E-mail auto-response and drip E-mail. Starting at $19/month for up to 500 E-mail addresses, you can import your current lists. Then you can:

- set up auto-responders
- set up drip campaigns
- send E-mail newsletters
- track campaign results, who opened E-mails, etc.
- even convert an RSS feed from your blogs or *Twitter* to E-mails

As your business grows and prospers, you'll want to spend less time managing things like E-mail, and less time monitoring performance for decisions. *AWeber* gives you the tools to make that happen.

iContact

Starting at $9.95 per month, *iContact (www.icontact.com)* also offers a number of useful E-mail features and services. The ability to track bounce-backs, opens and click-throughs to your offers is also a part of this service. From their site:

E-mail will be a large part of your marketing plan in the future, so look carefully at these and other services and select the one that most fully meets your needs. Don't short-change this area. In PPC and CPM, you're shooting for new prospects with no history, and you don't know if they'll buy or not. With those who you capture on these lists, you know their areas of interest and when/what they've purchased in the past. By segregating these recipients by product types or interest, you can do highly targeted E-mail offers in the future that will generate clicks and purchases.

Putting It All Together for Web sites

I've given you excellent tools here, and the knowledge you need, to get one or more Web sites up and generating income quickly. Whether you do a lot of it yourself, or you hire some, or all, of the work out, I've given you resources and links to make it happen for you.

- Hosting and domains
- Site design tools, software and freelancing
- Site content freelancing
- Affiliate marketing templates
- E-mail marketing from Web site leads
- My turnkey solution at *www.affiliatesystem.us* brings all of this in one solution

As we'll discuss next, whether you use Web sites, blogs or a combination of the two, you'll soon have all the knowledge you need.

Blogs

What is a Blog?

Blog, short for Weblog, refers to a type of Web site. A blog is a Web site as well, in the purest of definitions: a site on the Web. There are some major differences that may or may not be visible to the site visitor. The latest blog software packages, like *WordPress*, allow you to create a site that most visitors can't even tell is a blog-based site. What are the main differences?

What Works With Blogs

Blogs allow a more targeted approach to your marketing. You can determine current hot topics and trends, and blog about them. This brings a focused visitor to the site, and you're presenting precisely, and only, the material they wanted, with related offers.

You can also select your best converting offers for your blogging. By watching your conversion statistics from all of your offers on all platforms, you can locate opportunity in those that are converting best. These may justify dedicating a small blog focused on that product, offer or topic. This is taking a good conversion offer and making it convert even higher because you're focusing your blog content on it.

Blog about your highest payout offers. I'm talking about dollars per conversion here, rather than conversion rates. The fact that they pay you more also means that they're more costly to the consumer in most cases, so your conversion percentage may not be high. But if you're making $50, $100 or more from each conversion, the blog platform can be an excellent way to focus on this offer with content that will bring you more buyers.

Do a little of both. Find low payout offers that convert at high ratios, and blog about them. A million people looking for a low payout offer can bring you as much or more money than a high payout offer that only has a few thousand people searching for it at any given time.

How Content Displays

As we've just learned, there's a great deal of design that goes into displaying content on a regular Web site. It requires some HTML knowledge, as well as the use of tables to properly position content and images on the screen.

Blogs are essentially CMS, or *"Content Management Systems."* They allow the user to concentrate on creating written content with images, while the blog software does all of the display work. You are totally unconcerned with how the blog post or page will display, as it's a built-in feature of that blog's particular theme.

How Content is Arranged, Stored and Accessed

A regular Web site will require that you spend a great deal of time designing navigation (how visitors get around in the site). You'll have top or side buttons or text links to pages. Those pages will link out to sub-pages, and you'll need to set up buttons and links to make that happen as well. Then there are the sub-pages of the sub-page etc. Should you decide that you want to move a whole segment of content to a more user-friendly place on the site based on the subject matter or product, it's going to require changing these navigation links in multiple places. That's why all of the Web site design software packages have routines that check for dead links, or links that no longer point to any content because you moved or deleted it.

Blogs arrange content with links as well, but it's a very different structure that's largely managed for you. Using categories to group your blog posts (articles/pages) by subject matter, the blog software keeps similar content together, and displays it if requested by category. So, instead of worrying about how to make sure that you end up with a link from one of your pages to a post about an acai berry weight loss product, you will have assigned that post to the *"Acai Berry Products"* category when you wrote it. Calling up that category gets every post or article that's related. A benefit is that any post or article can have more than one category. So our acai berry post would show up in the acai berry category, as well as one for herbal products if we choose to group some of our content that way.

Why is this good for you? First, you are no longer wasting time trying to make sure that things end up where you want them on the site, and display in the way that you wanted. It just happens with a blog, so that you can concentrate on the content and selling your offers. Done right, your blog site can keep people engaged longer (stickyness), because it is easier to locate similar articles.

SEO, Search Engine Optimization

It is generally accepted that, unless you've been careful to hire a Web site designer with SEO skills, blogs inherently do better with the search engines. Many believe this is only because most blogs are posted very frequently and on a regular basis, thus getting the search engine robots to visit more often and increasing exposure. This is true, but there's another reason. As blogging software has improved, with *WordPress* on version 2.8 now (at least four versions after I started using it), the way that the blog software organizes content, directories, and names, your posts (articles) is more friendly to search engines. There are even plugins that are specifically designed for *WordPress* to increase search engine exposure and get better rankings.

Plugins

A plugin is a small piece of software added to a blog package to accomplish a specific task that isn't part of the basic blog software functionality. Plugins help in managing images, resizing images, changing display options for the site, enhancing SEO, placing third party functionality in the site to interact with other sites, and more.

Hosting and Blogs

I'll make it clear that all instructions and information here are for use on the self-hosted *WordPress* blog platform. It's best for the professional use of blogging, and it's inexpensive but powerful. So, though a great deal of this information will apply to *Joomla* or *Drupal* as well, many of the plugins and functionality may not be available. And, none of this can be accomplished on the free blogging platforms like *Blogger*.

Let's clear up the free and paid hosting versions of *WordPress* now, as it's important that you know the difference. *www.wordpress.com* is the place to start a totally free blog. You can get one up and running in minutes. It can be a good test to see at how *WordPress* works, but it isn't what you want for your marketing long-term. That's because free *Word-Press.com* sites are hosted there, which greatly limits your functionality and design options because they're paying for your space and bandwidth. It will be a nice site, BUT you can't:

- select from thousands of free and low cost "themes" that allow you to have the color schemes and site design you want (The free version gives you choices limited to a few basic themes).
- install super new functionality and design capabilities with third party plugins. What they give you is all you get, and it's not enough.
- there's more, but those are the two main issues. It's so cheap to host your own, there's simply no contest.

At *www.wordpress.org,* you get the help and resources for a powerful self-hosted blogging solution. But you don't need to go there to get started. This is where we get into the differences between hosting solutions.

Because it's a Web site, you can host a *WordPress* blog anywhere. But, there's a hitch. If the hosting provider doesn't give you an easy *WordPress* install utility, you practically have to become a programmer to get the software and associated databases properly installed on the host servers. The first two host solutions I gave you, *HostGator* and *BlueHost,* are where you should look first. *GoDaddy.com* and *Yahoo.com* also offer the same easy *WordPress* install.

Once you've set up your hosting account at one of these sites, you will find an option to install the complete *WordPress* package. Answer a few questions, and within minutes, you're looking at your *WordPress* dashboard, ready for you to get to work. The software and associated databases for storing your content are installed for you, you need only to select a theme and get ready to post.

Hosting and Blog Format Planning

There is more than one way to set up multiple blogs for your offers. You can use one hosting solution, just organizing things a bit differently depending on the offers you'll be placing.

1. A large blog with smaller offer blogs featuring related products or offers. An example might be a blog about weight loss, with smaller mini-blogs for subsets of products. This approach uses one *WordPress* installation, with one common theme. The mini-blogs for different product types or offers would have the same design, but you could use the *"categories"* option to group them easily for display together. Doing this (I'll show you how later) allows you to buy a domain name just for acai berry products, and point it at a category page for those products that the blog creates for you with your newest offers or articles/posts at the top.

2. Individual blogs with different themes is the second approach. These mini-blogs could even be a single page of posts specifically written to promote a single product or smaller group of similar products. You would need to do a separate *WordPress* install for each of these, as you'll be using different themes and designs.

Both of these approaches can be accomplished with the same hosting solution. It's just a different setup on the servers, and the host tech support staff can help you get it done right.

Themes and Blog Design

For the fastest and easiest start, just choose a theme designed specifically for affiliate marketing. These carry a cost, but usually aren't expensive, and the time saved can be worth a lot more to you. Also, the theme may have been around a while, proving its worth in CTR and conversions.

Though I'm not recommending this theme or site, an example of a theme advertised as specifically designed for affiliate marketing is at:

http://affiliatetheme.net

There are many others; you can compare them with a *Google* search for *"affiliate themes for wordpress,"* or a similar search. What you're gaining, if the theme is properly constructed, is a design that facilitates the fast placement of offers and images in a way that gets a click from the site visitor. There should also be some SEO built into the theme to help in affiliate marketing. Read their descriptive literature carefully, as once you've downloaded a theme, it's difficult to get a refund if it doesn't work for you. Some of the features you're looking for include:

- Easy way to change site colors with one operation for full site changes
- SEO considerations for PPC, CPM and normal SEO to get better positions and lower costs
- Choices for the home page and interior page layouts, with the ability to use different layouts for different offer types
- Customizable header graphics to better match the header image to the blog's content

Once you find a theme you like, check your licensing to see if you can use it on more than one site without buying another license. If you're planning a lot of smaller individual sites, this is an expensive approach.

Free Themes Will Work Well For You

If you enjoy looking at Web site designs, color schemes and similar features, you can have a wonderful time checking out *WordPress* themes. Their basic site with hundreds of free ones is at:

http://wordpress.org/extend/themes

There are some things to consider other than just "pretty" for your theme. The goal of the affiliate marketing blog is to make money from clicks through to your offers. The layout of blog themes can have a big impact on conversions.

The Number of Columns

WordPress themes come in a number of column formats. Almost all have a main column where content is displayed. We'll call that the one-column format (though there aren't really any, and we wouldn't want one anyway).

Then, side columns are added. A two-column theme would have the main column, plus an additional column, either on the right or left side. Here's an example:

In this theme, the side column is on the right. So, there are two columns; one wide and one narrow. Now, in most cases, the content in the narrow column stays the same no matter what page you're on. You can place navigation there, so that your offer links would be the same on every page.

Next are three and four column themes; more columns means more flexibility in displaying what you want, where you want. Also, many themes allow for changing the content of some columns for different pages, as well as custom plugins for ads. Here is a screen shot of a three and a four column theme.

You can begin to see that the possibilities are almost limitless, with thousands of free themes out there. Other important considerations:

- Which columns can change based on the page, and which always show the same content
- If you want buttons at the top of your site for some navigation, make sure you choose a theme that has them
- You can always put page navigation into one of the columns
- Make sure it says that it is *"widget ready."* (A widget is a plugin)
- Can you change the header image with a custom one?
- The header image and any large images near the top are actually big space wasters. You want your ads *"above the fold"* (before scrolling downward), so wasting space on an image that doesn't generate income is not desirable.

You can see that there are many choices and the limitations aren't great. You can upload multiple themes to your site, testing several, since you can change themes with one click and change the whole site.

Do Split Tests of Multiple Themes & Colors

We assume that we know what will work in getting that click from the blog visitor. But the truth is that people react in unexpected ways at times, and we need to place our advertising out there in multiple formats and styles to test for the best performers. Free *WordPress* themes open up possibilities, because we're not spending money to test.

Use three or four different themes and/or color schemes to test a blog's performance. You could have a couple running, changing the theme after a week or so to see how a different theme, design or color palette pulls for you. Does this work? I can give an example from my own experience. I recently put up a blog to market one of my affiliate offers. I used a purple background and ran it for three days. In a couple of days, I was showing a net loss of almost $1,000. The third day I changed the background color to pink. I'm now tripling my advertising investment each day!

Content – It's Your Product Here

You're advertising the products of others, but you're doing it with your product…content. Blogs have become so popular and powerful for business because they are conversations and instruction tools, not just a static display of product literature. People will come to your blog, stay there a while, and return again, if they find content that is valuable to them.

Using our popular weight loss product category as an example again, what would bring visitors to your blog, and how would they find it? I went to *Google*'s keyword tool and entered these three search phrases:

- weight loss
- lose weight
- weight and health

I got pages of results, scanning them for opportunities both in the number of searches and the competition for the words and phrases. Here are some that I liked for possible future posts to the blog:

- effective weight loss
- fast weight loss
- lose weight/fat

- lose fat
- lose pounds
- weight management
- lose lbs

This is an interesting list, as the last four items were suggested by *Google*, and they really didn't contain all of my words or a combination of them. Let's look at each, and how a blog post article might take advantage of them.

I'll use "effective weight loss" as an example. Getting 30,000+ clicks per month, this one isn't a big volume phrase, but lends itself to several posts that caution about claims that aren't real, allowing you to present your product offers with some type of validation of results. Post titles like *"Effective Weight Loss is Weight That Stays Off,"* or combining it with *"fast weight loss,"* a phrase getting 200,000 clicks per month with a title like *"Effective Weight Loss Isn't Always Fast Weight Loss."*

"Lose weight/fat" – This one gets more than 20,000 clicks per month, and I wouldn't have thought that this combination was even entered. This makes competition less fierce, and it would lead well into a post titled *"Weight Isn't All Fat – Be Careful of Lose Weight/Fat Claims."* A simple post about the components of weight, muscle and fat would get you some traffic for example, *"lose pounds."* Getting one million clicks per month, this one could take a health tone, with *"lose pounds with care,"* or *"lose pounds not your health,"* or combining with the last one *"weight management,"* we could do an article/post titled *"Lose Pounds With Sensible Weight Management."*

These are just suggestions, with the important goal of selecting search phrases related to our offer, working with those with high search volume, and/or lower competition. Then we craft a post idea around the phrase. Then we write it, or we hire someone to write them for us.

Elance and *Guru* for Blog Posts

I gave you an introduction to these two freelance sites in the chapter on Web sites. All of that information applies, but we can add a bit to it that's more specific to blogs and bloggers. For some reason, the buyers of content on these sites tend to de-value blogging in comparison to writing Web content or Web articles. There's really no rational reason to consider blog posts as easier to write, or of less value than articles of other types.

Words are words, and a good writer will write good blog posts, while a bad one will…well, you know.

Maybe this bias comes from the fact that most effective blog posts aren't very wordy, with a great many of them in lengths between 100 and 300 words. There are also millions of them under 100 words, trying to create a baiting post to get a click to something more substantial in the way of content. The problem with too short a post is that your key phrase doesn't get enough exposure for you to get a reasonable quality score on your PPC or CPM accounts.

Short isn't bad, but requires meaty content that gets the information across with optimization of your key phrase considered. Using our weight loss phrases above, we would hire a writer on *Elance* or *Guru*, and give them a list of titles, with a brief description of what we want if the title isn't self-explanatory. Tell them to optimize for your phrase. Give them an approximate word count for posts.

A great many blog posts are purchased on these freelance sites for as little as $2 each for 200-400 words. This is tricky, because the better writers are getting $0.05/word or more, making posts of this length more in the range of $10-$20 each. In all likelihood, you'll be able to get good content close to the lower figure, but be careful. Look at samples of the bidders' work and set clear expectations in your project description.

It's also OK to have them write two or more variations of every post, discounting you for the word count. You get more content that you can place on multiple test blogs, or just multiple long-term blogs, each bringing in the clicks.

Offer Placement

I've already mentioned the term *"above the fold"* for ad placement. In the print world, this means on the top half of the newspaper, before they have to flip to see the bottom. In our Internet world, it's before they have to scroll downward to view content. And don't forget that there are many different screen sizes out there, from giant desktop screens to mini net books with 10 inch screens.

Keep as many ads as possible high on the page, so they are definitely seen, even if the visitor doesn't scroll down at all. But don't forget that many do scroll down to view older blog posts or more information. So, place the same or modified offers again, lower on the page as well. You want one or more ads visible no matter where the visitor is on the page.

RSS Feeds, E-mail & Newsletters for Blogs

RSS feeds came into their own with blogs, and they're now a standard part of every *WordPress* theme. You don't need to do anything to create one for your *WordPress* blog, as it is part of the basic structure. You just need to place the URL feed link anywhere you want to offer a subscription for your feed to your site visitors. This can be done in a number of ways, including just a text link like *"Subscribe to my blog's news feed here."* The link is to the feed URL, which you'll find in your blog's setup in multiple places. There will be the orange icon, as well as a widget called *"Meta Data"* that has a link to your main RSS feed.

What you need to remember is that sources tell us that less than 10% of the population knows what a RSS feed is, or uses the news readers to get the feed. So, we're missing up to 90+% of our prospect audience for sub-scriptions if this is all we offer. No problem; there are plugins and widgets available to send out an E-mail of each post to subscribers, so they can subscribe via E-mail as well. Most will choose this, as they understand it and use E-mail every day.

Another RSS tool you'll want to keep in mind for use is the fact that *WordPress* creates a feed for every category in your blog, besides the feed for all content. So, if one of your strategies is to build a large blog about weight loss, with categories for different types of products, such as acai berry, and for diets and other break-outs of your offers, you will end up a RSS feed for each of these categories.

If you have a feed just for acai berry, you can have subscribers for your blog or the automated newsletter will show you, and they can target their subscription to the content they want. This is great for you as well, as you can then create an automated newsletter from that feed, with subscribers only interested in one facet of your large weight loss site.

Subscription Options

One of the hundreds of widgets that you can locate for your blogs is one that displays like this:

This one has three buttons, the orange icon universally used for RSS feeds, an E-mail subscription envelope icon, and even a link to follow me on *Twitter*. When you install the widget, you give it the links for each button in setup and it creates this linking sidebar item for you. All you have to do is place it where you want it in one of your sidebars.

This is a good way to do it, as it's pretty compact in your sidebar display. By keeping a lot above the fold, you'll be continuously concerned with your screen "real estate." When you can clearly communicate what you want the visitor to do, as this one does, in a smaller space, it's a better choice than larger plugins.

The Automated Newsletter Option

As most of your subscribers will be via E-mail, you'll be creating a newsletter, and the best approach is one that takes up little of your time, but looks professionally produced. One option is to altogether avoid E-mail subscriptions that send one post at a time. Instead, you will send a weekly or monthly (your choice) newsletter.

A service that is inexpensive and works well for this is *Feedblitz* (*www. feedblitz.com*). You can create multiple newsletters here for different blogs, but your subscription cost is based on the number of E-mail addresses in your lists. There is a free account option, but there are limitations that change, so check it out for your needs. In the current paid version, for up to 1,000 E-mail addresses, the cost is $13.95/month. So, how does this automated newsletter work?

Once you set up your *Feedblitz* account, you upload your E-mail lists, and then you create your newsletter(s). You can customize colors, fonts and logos. Then, you just give *Feedblitz* your RSS feed for the blog. If you've elected a weekly newsletter on a Tuesday for example, at one minute after midnight Monday, *Feedblitz* checks your RSS feed, grabbing all new posts since the last newsletter the week before. It creates the newsletter, images and text, and sends it out. It doesn't get any easier, and it's an effective ongoing communication tool to pitch new offers to your subscribers by posting about them.

In the three button subscriber plugin above, we would just place the link to the *Feedblitz* subscription page as the destination when they click on the E-mail envelope icon. This page allows the visitor to subscribe in various ways, as well as handling all E-mail opt-in and unsubscribe activities to keep us legal.

Plugins and Widgets

Here is a great time to talk about plugins and widgets for *WordPress*, as this is how you'll end up placing many of your ads, subscription boxes, and offers on the page. They are normally placed in the side columns, left or right of the main content posts. They give you awesome flexibility to present your offers next to relevant content, as well as to feature other content elsewhere, and link to your other blogs, Web sites, *Facebook*, *Twitter* and other online presences.

Not long ago, *WordPress* celebrated its 100,000th plugin. That's amazing, considering 95% plus of these are absolutely free for use on your blogs. If you're sitting around wishing you could accomplish something new on your blog, there's probably a plugin that will get it done. The developer community is huge. There are plugins out there to:

- speed up the loading of your pages
- improve your blog's SEO
- display your tweets
- display RSS feeds in sidebars (side columns) and even as excerpts on a page
- display *Google* ads, *Adbrite* and others
- show avatars of your visitors and subscribers
- many, many, many more

There is almost nothing you'll think of that you can't accomplish with a good plugin. What about your display ads from your affiliate network? This is probably the easiest task you'll have. First, depending on the width of the column on your blog, you select the appropriate ad display size. Then, copy out the code the site gives you. Drag the "text" widget to the sidebar column in your *WordPress* dashboard. Then paste in the ad code. Within minutes, you have a display ad in one of your sidebars. Dragging the ads is simple to get them in the order and position you want.

Two Plugins to Make Images Easier

Your advertisers will supply you with visual ads, including images, which will have the code to display the image appropriately. However, when we're building Web sites and posting to blogs, a bit of color and a photo now and then adds to the professional look of our site. Too much text without a break for color can turn your visitor away.

There are two plugins that make images easy and fast with *WordPress*, neither requiring you to upload the image to your site, as the regular *WordPress* image insert does.

Flickr

If you use *Flickr* for images, this plugin ties your *WordPress* blog to your *Flickr* account, allowing you to insert an image from any of your *Flickr* collections or sets with just one click.

Zemanta

Zemanta.com, (http://zemanta.com) allows you to set up a free account, and then upload, install and activate their plugin. This is a great one, as you don't need any images of your own. Once you have the plugin, *Zemanta* resides in your sidebar next to where you're writing a new post. It reads your post content, and suggests images tagged with keywords related to what you've written. All you have to do is understand the licenses (explanation at *Zemanta* or *http://creativecommons.org*), and select any that are appropriately licensed for your use. Here's what *Zemanta* looks like for a post about llamas on a blog:

FirstRSS Plugin for Updated Free Content

One plugin you'll want to get is *FirstRSS*. This allows you to enter the RSS feed URL for any blog, and your page will display excerpts of the posts there. Here's a screen shot of a *Topix.com* news feed for a certain area: This is ready-made content that can be very tightly focused on the offers

you're promoting on that page. And don't forget our previous example of using *Google* alerts to create a feed alert system for us. Think of the power you get with this setup.

- Do a *Google* Alert on *"health and weight loss"* as an example
- Get the RSS feed for this alert
- Place that feed in your post or page

- You get a constant feed of new material on your topic and related to your offers

The greatest value of this plugin is that it isn't limiting your display to the sidebars, as most all other RSS feed plugins do. The content is part of the page or post. It can be the entire one page blog if you want!

Wait, there's more! Let's think about using this plugin to create a page that is nothing but good commentary on *Twitter* about acai berry. You go to *Twitter* search, and enter the search query as *"acai berry")* and the smiley face should pull tweets with positive words about acai berry. If you were doing the opposite, promoting an alternative to weight loss with acai berry products, you'd just change the smiley face to a frown.

Next to your search results, you'll see the orange RSS feed icon and the text *"feed for this query."* Just right click and copy out the link, which looks like this:

http://search.twitter.com/search.atom?q=acai+berry+%3A%29

Use this feed with the *FirstRSS* plugin, and you have a page full of rapidly updating positive tweets about "acai berry."

This strategy of using *Google* Alert and *Twitter* feeds for page content will definitely result in other affiliate marketing links in the alerts and posts. How effective the strategy ends up being will have a lot to do with how you word and position your ads on the page. After all, the visitor is there, and there may be a link in the news item or alert that will take them to another site with an offer. Your offer is right there in front of them, before that outgoing click happens. Get their attention with a great ad, and the click is yours. The tradeoff for the risk of lost visitors is the easy and free content that is updated for you by users all over the Web.

Category and Domain Name Site Creation

I told you earlier how to buy domain names, and how you can point them to any page on the Web. This leads to a little strategy for creating mini-sites from *WordPress* blog categories. In our weight loss example, we have categories for our articles and posts such as:

- Diets
- Diet Books
- Health and Weight Loss
- Acai Berry

We've written or purchased posts and articles focused around key phrases in these categories. The *"Health and Weight Loss"* category has a number of posts focused on the health aspects of weight loss plans, diets and products. This category will have its own RSS feed maintained by *WordPress*. You need to understand how category pages are created by *WordPress* now. Every time a category page is called for display, it is dynamically created right then, with the newest posts at the top, and posts listed down the main column.

So, if someone calls for this category from a link on the blog home page, they will be presented with a page created right then, with the very latest posts at the top. Now, this could be a completely separate site with all the setup and maintenance that goes with it, and you might want to take that approach. But if time, income and other considerations require a different approach, this category strategy will work well for you.

The visitor has called for this category page, so they're seeing a list of posts related to health issues and weight loss. How can we enhance this? We can purchase a domain name, hopefully with *"health and weight loss"* in it. Then, we just point that domain at this category page URL. We get the URL by going to the page and copying it out of the address bar at the top. Now, anyone going to our domain name. (perhaps *"healthandweightlossfactors.com")* will come to this category page with all of the information focused on this topic.

The only problem with our offers and ads in this strategy is that our sidebars are displaying the offers we've placed there, whether they're precisely related to the content of this category page or not. So, you'll want to work some of your specific offers into your posts here. Using affiliate offer links out of the posts will get the clicks you need.

E-mail Marketing to your Blog Visitors

The automated newsletter strategy is a great way to follow up with E-mail marketing to those who subscribe to your blog with E-mail. However, many won't do this, so what's another way to grow your lists? It's the same as with your Web site's free reports. You can use the same reports you may be using elsewhere on the Web, or create new ones. Use an *Elance* or *Guru* writer if necessary to create custom reports you can offer to your blog visitors.

Once you have the report, you create an auto-responder for delivery, just like with a Web site. The form to get their E-mail address is easily placed with the text box widget we talked about earlier. Place the code for the report offer via E-mail, and you're done.

This is just one example of how you can catch the eye of the visitor with the symbol. Deliver your report with all of your associated offers, and you're on your way to immediate income, as well as ready to market to this prospect again with E-mail in the future.

Give & Take with Social Media

Depending on your goals for each blog and your social media presence, you can use RSS feeds and plugins to display your social media information on your blog, or your blog posts on social sites, or both.

By using plugins, some actually supplied by the social sites themselves, you can place links to your profiles on *Twitter*, *MySpace*, *Facebook* and *LinkedIn*. Besides the value of the link to promote your social site presence, you could end up with other business from visitors who take these links to your profiles and find other information about you there, or about your other sites.

Facebook, *LinkedIn* and other social sites offer you the ability to feed your blog RSS feed to the site, showing your latest posts in your profile. Of course, the post display links them back to your blog, which works well for both SEO and income. This is how the author of one of the plugins to display posts on *Facebook* illustrates his plugin:

Here's a screen shot of the display one plugin shows your visitor which gives them links to connect to you all over the Internet. It's all about visibility and getting your sites and offers promoted everywhere you can. You never know how someone may stumble across you on the Web, so being visible everywhere possible is what you want.

A Quick Overview of *WordPress* Dashboard Functions

There are plenty of tutorials out there for using *WordPress*, and there is a great deal of help available from the user community at *WordPress.org*. However, just to give you a comfort level with using *WordPress*, here are some screen shots of the "behind-the-scenes" stuff you'll be doing.

This is a portion of the dashboard you see when you log in to work on your blog. Most of the boxes you see here can be moved around and customized. The boxes on the right are information relating to the main dashboard screen, telling you about new *WordPress* developments and plugins, as well as presenting you with your visitor and page view stats if you've activated the *WordPress* "*Stats Plugin.*"

Adding a new post is a lot like working in your favorite word processing software, with WYSIWYG functionality. You enter your title, then the body text. Buttons at the top of the body area allow you to change fonts and other text options, insert tables and images, and even forms if you like.

Your available themes are displayed for selection, and you can change from one to the other easily for testing.

Using plugins and widgets is as easy as dragging them from the *"available"* section on the left to the appropriate sidebar on the right. Then, you just drag them around on the right to put them in the order you want.

There's a lot more, but these screen shots should show you that *Word-Press* is very intuitive and easy to use, so don't be concerned about your abilities. You can do this.

The Blog Platform – Putting it All Together

It's easy to see from the information I've given you here why so many affiliate marketers are using blogs for a major portion of their Web marketing.

- Very inexpensive to host
- Easy content creation
- Very little site design required
- Ease in updating and adding content
- Automated content possibilities
- SEO value

Get started by checking out hosting providers who offer *WordPress* install as a free option. Then check out themes, both the free variety and ones designed especially for affiliate marketing. Use the criteria I taught you to choose a theme with the right structure for your content and offers.

Write regular and focused blog posts, or hire someone to write them for you. Careful project descriptions and bidder selection can get you a lot of content at low cost through *Elance.com* and *Guru.com*. Be sure that you have checked feedback, references and sample work of the bidders. Thoroughly describe your project, give examples, and detail of what you need. There is no such thing as too much information in a project description.

Use plugins and widgets for your ads and offers, and place direct links and advertisement image links directly into your posts. Keep as many ads and offers as possible *"above the fold."* But also place them farther down on the page, maybe even repeating offers. This way, no matter where they are on the page, offers are there to click.

Use your RSS feeds to advantage. Though 90% or so don't know how to use a RSS feed, you can create E-mail notifications from them as well. The E-mail automated newsletter strategy is killer. Creating custom and highly focused E-mail lists from subscription widgets and special report widgets will bring you profits from future marketing of offers to an established group with an interest.

Success Story # 7 – Robert Dickerson

Robert says: "Anthony Morrison taught me what he knows about making money online. So far I have been able to make a little over $500, and I just got started! The best thing about it is that it's easy, and it really works!

CHAPTER 3

Review Sites

People are followers for the most part. Particularly when they're spending money in tough times, they want to assure themselves that they're making a good decision. The best way to do that is to see what other people are saying, assuming that enough positive information indicates that they can purchase a product or service with some assurance of value.

There is also the equally powerful desire to avoid pain and problems. Instead of trying to make sure they are making a good decision, they very much want to avoid making a bad one, with mediocre being OK. There is a search for information that's BAD about a product or service, justifying a decision NOT to buy.

The Internet has honed the process to a high degree, with the presence of hundreds of thousands of Web sites and blogs dedicated to consumer comment and reviews of products and services. It would be difficult to impossible not to be able to locate positive and negative information about any company or their products, just by typing in a search phrase, or the company name in *Google*, *Yahoo*, *MSN* or other search engines.

The *Twitter* Good/Bad Search

Once *Twitter* hit the Web, social networking with 140 characters has become a huge phenomenon. We've already talked a great deal about *Twitter* as a marketing tool and an information resource. But there's more as it relates to review sites and affiliate marketing.

You can go to *http://search.twitter.com* and type in a company name, product, service or any phrase, follow it with **:)** and you'll get mostly positive comments about the company, product or search phrase. Entering it again as **:(** you'll get comments that have negative content.

This is based on the presence of certain words and phrases in the content of the Tweet, and isn't perfect. But it points out that there is enough of interest to locate public comments about almost anything or anybody. Whether the comment is positive or negative, *Twitter* search techniques have evolved to fill the need.

Another approach to content using the *Twitter* universe has already been presented. That's using a *Twitter* search feed with the *FirstRSS* plugin to generate a page of related and constantly updated tweets about your blog subject. Combining this approach with the positive and negative searches we just mentioned, you can gather positive comments about a product, and just use the feed to create another page on your blog with offers. Test to see if it works.

If you want to avoid any links that might go to a competitor, we will not want to just display the feed of the *Twitter* search. Instead, take a few minutes each day to check that search and click on the links. If they are good opinions or reviews, and they aren't to competitive offers, it is worth your time to just enter the text of that tweet and the link to it in a short blog post. You needn't say any more than *"I found another happy user of XXXX today."* Link that text to the tweet. It's fresh content with the product name in it for a relevant link.

Review Sites Provide a Needed Service

Obviously, what we need as affiliate marketers is the click for income. But, what our review sites do for the consumer is what will bring the site visitors. Basically, a review site is one that offers reviews, or opinions, about products and services. These can be your own opinions, or those of others you gather around the Web.

Of course, if you have personal knowledge about the product or service, it makes for easier and faster review site creation, but it isn't necessary. You have the resources on the Web to locate informed opinion of others, and even expert tests or evaluations. When you do this, you can offer your review as a statement of information you have gathered. It's still valid information, especially if coming from a formal study or academic activity.

You Don't Care What Decision They Make

Taking a currently popular example, let's examine the content and offers for a site reviewing free credit report offers. Any time there are a lot of Web pages pushing a product or service, interest caused the creation of those pages. Interest generated simply because they're now out there competing for attention and business. They generate their own "*buzz.*"

So, you create a simple review site that contains your commentary on a group of these free credit report offer sites and their services. Your review material can come from:

- your own personal past experience with the offers
- some tests you run yourself, subscribing to the offers to see what you get
- research you do on the Web for valid commentary by others with some authority

Now, you do care that your material is factual or a correct statement of opinion. But you don't care what decision the consumer may make from reading the material and comparing the offers from your reviews. You will have all of the reviewed offers available there for their choice and click. You will get your payout no matter which they choose.

This is valid; as you really don't know any single visitor's needs, nor do you know which particular offer might mention a service or feature that's important to them. You've rendered a service by contrasting and comparing the offers, and allowed the visitor to make their choice with more information at their disposal.

The visitor is most likely on your review site because they haven't yet made a decision. If you do a good job with your reviews, then the visitor are very likely to make that decision right there, clicking through to one of your offers, and getting you your payout.

The Mechanics of the Review Site

The blog format or platform lends itself well to the goals of a review site. We need to keep our review site focused on one subject, as we're bringing a targeted audience to the site. We'll need multiple sites, each developed around this one subject or product/service type.

We'll also want to do some testing, with more than one site about the same subject. We'll test format, design, colors, offers and offer placement on our free credit report offers across two or more sites. Doing this will allow us to make changes and settle in on one or two that produce the income we need from our marketing efforts and expense.

We've already determined that low costs, with generous space and bandwidth allowances, make hosting a large number of sites affordable. With our *WordPress* software installs as part of the package at no extra cost, blogs become the logical and best approach to review site marketing. We can have a great number of blogs hosted in one place, with fast setup and easy content creation.

One advantage we have in using our *WordPress* blogs is that our split testing will eventually yield certain themes and color schemes that seem to always work for certain product and service offers. Once we know what they are, the ability to simply select our theme again with one click will help us to get these multiple sites online more efficiently.

In the simplest of formats, your site may be one single blog post or page, with a listing of the offers, products or services, and your review of each. You can offer your visitor fast and easy click-through to all of the reviewed offers via direct links from the text of the review, and strategically placed offers in the sidebars next to each review.

Once your site is up and bringing in visitors, don't rest on your past efforts. One of the things that make a blog so SEO effective is regular new content so you should post as often as you can, adding new information you learn or dig out on the Web.

Using the *"Sticky Post"* to your Advantage

WordPress now gives you the ability to *"stick"* a post to the top of the home page. In many cases, you may only have one page sites, so this allows you to keep one post at the top, while those below it will sort with the newest at the top. This means that your sticky post could have been written a month ago, but it will stay on the top. The posts you've written since will be below it, with the newest one on the top.

If the content of one post is more *"evergreen,"* meaning long lasting in effectiveness, then you could stick it to the top. You could mention in that post to keep scrolling for new information, sales offers and freebies. This isn't always going to be the way you want to lay out the site, but if it works for one site, and then it's free and easy to do with *WordPress*.

Offers and Freebies for Getting E-mail Addresses

We're always trying to get more than just a click through to an offer and a single payout. We also want to get as many E-mail addresses as possible, building highly targeted E-mail lists for future marketing and E-mailing of offers specifically geared toward the past interests displayed by the visitor. Here are some ideas for getting those E-mail addresses:

- free short reports or one page informational packages on the subject
- buy something inexpensive from *eBay* (with resale rights) and give it away to those who give up that E-mail address
- create an "*expert advice*" file on the topic that is free via E-mail
- create a contest giveaway, an *iPod*, executive pen, or other item. People love freebies, so they'll give you their E-mail address to enter
- membership for exclusive early notice of future reviews or special offers

As I told you before, keep these offers above the fold, and use easy E-mail forms from *AWeber* or your chosen auto-responder provider. If the page requires scrolling for more information, you can place offers lower, but make them repeats, or at least place the best payouts at the top. Here's where the three or four column blog format helps, by giving you more sidebar area to work with.

Remember that just a review of the offer or product isn't enough. Create a CTA, or Call To Action. You need to tell the visitor what to do, not assume that they'll know or automatically take the action you want. A CTA will increase your CTR to your offers.

Using Freelancers to Build Your Review Site

Using *Elance.com* and *Guru.com*, you can place projects to design multiple *WordPress* sites. There are a large number of blog site designers on these sites, and once you set out your criteria, you can even give them a login to actually do all of the setup for you. Because there's a lot of replication, you should be able to negotiate a price that is worth the savings in time for you.

An interesting side note about logins: never give out your admin login to outside designers or writers. You will frequently be hiring writers to post directly to your blogs as well. Direct posting is more efficient than having them E-mail you a copy that you must then paste into the blog and format. The solution: always create a login specifically for each provider. This way, once they've completed their project, you can delete their login.

Freelancers with Niche Knowledge

You can search the freelance sites for providers with specific knowledge related to the products or services you're about to promote with offers. Though they may be a little more expensive, you might find that the content is better, and they can even do some of the review text, with your guidance to be positive about the offer. A professional writer can write positively or negatively about any topic, placing their personal viewpoints aside.

Also, you'll want to offer blogging packages as longer term steady work if you can. Writers on the freelance sites expend a great deal of overhead time in reading projects, bidding work, monitoring bids, and billing out the work. They will always gravitate to project titles that mention long-term or ongoing blog posts. They'll compromise on their pricing in exchange for agreed-upon billing over a longer period. You can do the escrow deposits in smaller increments, never having too much out there if you decide to cancel a project.

Review Sites Make Money

There are a number of reasons why review sites are profitable for the affiliate marketer:

1. They are built around a topic or product/service, bringing targeted visitors.
2. Visitors are trying to make a decision, searching for the opinion of others.

3. Multiple related offers are presented, with money made no matter which they choose.
4. They are fast and inexpensive to build.

Make review sites one facet of your affiliate marketing plan. Their topic focus, while presenting alternatives make them less *"sales-pushy,"* and more consumers helpful, generating those money clicks for you.

CHAPTER 4

The Direct Linking Marketing Platform

We've been progressing through our four models roughly in order of how effective they are in generating business; though blogs and Web sites are pretty much equal. Direct linking is an effective way to generate income because it is really easy to do. The trade-off is that your CTR from direct linking is pretty low.

Direct linking is placing links directly to your advertiser offer sites, rather than bringing visitors to your sites first for some pre-selling. You place these links all over the Web, from article sites to *CraigsList,* to forums, blogs and message boards.

What are the Cons?

1. By taking the prospect directly to the advertiser's site, you lose the ability to pre-sell on one of your sites.
2. PPC and CPM can't be used, as the search engines will not allow you to promote a link to a site that you don't own.
3. It's more difficult to measure results, as the visitor isn't going through one of your control points first.

What are the Pros?

1. You aren't losing a prospect on one of your sites before they see the advertiser's sale page or sign up/purchase form. They go directly there.
2. With a higher percentage of those who click actually seeing the advertiser's offer, conversion percentages can be higher if the advertiser does a good job.

It certainly is easy to place these links around the Web if you're going to places where this particular topic, product or service is being discussed, and you're placing a short amount of text with the link directly to the advertiser's site and offer/form. You can increase your income here simply by being careful how you comment, and what you say on the various sites and forums where you'll be posting. Many of them are moderated, and will delete your entry if it is blatant selling.

Your goal here is to add relevance and value to the conversation, wherever it is. If your comment adds insight to the discussion, it will be allowed to stay, and will generate clicks for you along the way. This isn't difficult, as you do have knowledge about the products and services you promote.

A comment can be as simple as, *"Though I haven't yet tried Brand XX, they're running a special offer here that I think I'll give a try."* You're not participating here with an E-mail address that connects with the advertiser, nor pointing to one of your sites. It is very possible that you're a consumer who is about to jump on a good offer. Others who see your comment may want to try it as well.

This strategy is related to our previous information about review sites, and how people look for validation from others to make a positive decision, or warnings from others to avoid a bad choice. How about *"After I got a speeding ticket racing to return a rented video, I tried Netflix, and I love it. They have a $1.99 one month trial here."* That link just may make you some money depending on where you placed it.

Message Boards and Forums

All through this book, whether we've been discussing SEO, PPC, CPM, or just placement of offers and site content, we've mentioned "relevance" many times. The Web has created huge clique groups of people focused on discussion of common interests. There are forums and discussion groups by the thousands all over the Web. They have a central topic of interest, and the members are sharing information that they all find of some value.

Yahoo Groups

A search at *http://groups.yahoo.com* on *"weight loss,"* sorted by number of members yields "*ThyroidNews*" as the top group, with almost 28,000 members, and this group is ten years old. You get a description of each group's interest, how old it is, how many members, and more.

Google Groups

Similar to *Yahoo Groups*, *Google Groups* (http://groups.*google*.com) is a bit more difficult to navigate and locate what you want. However, FAQ's and other features that make commenting and direct linking fruitful.

CraigsList.com

This one is pretty obvious, as craigslist.com was formed to promote classified ads free to consumers. With the ability to target areas and subject matter with keywords and phrases, you can place your direct linking ads all over this resource. Of course, the competition is doing the same thing, so be creative to get better CTR.

Your Own E-mail Signatures

Throughout this book, for every marketing platform, we've been strongly supporting building focused E-mail lists for follow-up marketing. There should never be an E-mail going out in a promotion to one of these lists without a relevant offer direct link in your E-mail signature. The more relevant the offer, and the text of the link, the better.

This isn't as big of a logistic headache as you might think. Just use *Microsoft NotePad*, *Word*, or other software, and build signature files all in a row, with each having a different offer link. Group them by product or offer type. When you're about to send out an E-mail, just copy and paste the best signature. You might even break up the E-mail promotion into more than one group, with different signatures for each as a test of offers and link text.

This is an excellent direct linking strategy; you are targeting a group who has already expressed an interest in this subject, product or service. Even if you're promoting a main offer in the E-mail, or several of them, they may not have an interest. So try to use a different offer and text in the E-mail signature. It gives them another choice and you another chance at a click.

Bringing It ALL Together

You're at the end of this book, but at the beginning of a new financially secure life. All you have to do is to follow the plans, implement the platforms, and use the tools I've given you here. It's a lot of information, because knowledge is what will make you successful. Everything you need for success is here. Just go back through the book, and follow these steps and use the tools I've given you.

You *CAN* do this

We started out with the statement that all you need to make it happen for you is the motivation and desire. I've given you the knowledge and tools. Blue collar, stay-at-home parent, office worker, traveling sales person, or any other job you have, you can do this in the time you have. I began by telling you about my business that bought a hot tub at the age of seven. It isn't intelligence, education or age.

You don't need any office space, or even a computer, as you can use computers at coffee houses, libraries, or anywhere else. You don't need a job. After all, if you've lost your job, you now have the time others do not to build your affiliate marketing business faster.

The Five Personality Components of Entrepreneurial Thinking

You've gotten this far in this book, so you started with the first two components: **Motivation** and **Resourcefulness**. The material I've shared with you here, **Knowledge** and **Strategies** take care of all but one. The last, **Confidence**, comes from bringing the other four together, and trusting your abilities to follow the instructions.

Affiliate Marketing Isn't Retail nor Is It Selling

We compared the huge start-up costs for a retail business with the minimal costs to get your affiliate marketing business up and generating income. This is one of the last and greatest frontiers, with a gold rush going on right now. Your wagon is now out in front just because you have the knowledge presented here.

What it is & How it Works

I explained affiliate marketing to you. We learned that it's one of the few business endeavors where everyone involved is working for your success. The advertiser wants you to succeed, and your affiliate network and your affiliate manager are dedicated to helping you to make lots of money, as they succeed only if you do. We looked at the best affiliate networks and how they function.

You learned how to negotiate a better deal for yourself, even when you're brand new to the business. They want you to succeed, but this is business after all. You'll never be offered the best deal out of the box. I've given you the strategies and words to negotiate top payouts from day one.

The Structure and Terminology

You know how your compensation is derived, how the ads and offers work, all about CPL, CPA, CTR, and the various ways that offers can be structured. You learned how the type of offer, cost, and actions required of the consumer can influence your income.

Learning these terms and offer structure information will help you to evaluate offers and select the ones that work best for you, increasing your income dramatically in the process.

PPC and CPM Marketing

Your advertising to get visitors to your many sites will consist in large part of PPC and CPM marketing. I've shown you how they work, where to go to get them started, how to structure your campaigns, and how to structure your sites, ads and content to increase your CTR, while getting better positions at a lower cost.

You have received detailed instruction in ad creatives, what works, how to get them designed, where to place each type of creative, and how to test and measure results.

The Platforms and Tools

Once you get the visitor to one of your marketing platforms, it must be properly designed and positioned to get that all-important next action – the money click. I've taken you through the four platforms that bring you income: **Web sites, Blogs, Review Sites,** and **Direct Linking.** You know where to host your sites, how to evaluate hosting, how to get domain names, and what the best of each platform looks like.

A great many tools that will bring your sites to successful Web presences are all here. I've given you the tools to get the best sites and blogs up, but at low cost. You've received specific instructions on hiring freelance help. These tips will help you to get better content at lower writing and design costs than those who don't know the ropes.

Don't miss out on the success others have enjoyed:

Dan M. – The drywall finisher who, in his fifties, was able to start generating income in the first week or two.

Halie – A work-at-home Mom with two boys who is watching her income grow every month.

Adrian – Received a $75,000 check last month, has $150,000 in savings, owns a new Jaguar and an Escalade…at age 24.

Justin K – At 26 years of age, he's generated over $1 million using what Anthony taught him. He paid cash for his first home.

The success stories keep coming, and we'd like to hear yours after you've taken what you have learned here and started your successful Internet business.

You're ending a book and beginning a business. I won't say "good luck," as you don't need it.

Index